A Consuming Fire
Encounters with Elie Wiesel and the Holocaust

D1505194

Other Books by John K. Roth

Freedom and the Moral Life, 1969
The Moral Philosophy of William James (ed.), 1969
Problems of the Philosophy of Religion, 1971
The Philosophy of Josiah Royce (ed.), 1971
The Moral Equivalent of War and Other Essays (ed.), 1971
The American Religious Experience (with Frederick Sontag), 1972
American Dreams, 1976
God and America's Future (with Frederick Sontag), 1977

a consuming fire

fire

Encounters with Elie Wiesel and the Holocaust

JOHN K. ROTH

Prologue by Elie Wiesel

JOHN KNOX PRESS
ATLANTA

s are from the Revised Standard Version
1971, 1973 by the Division of Christian
Education, National Council of the Churches of Christ in the U.S.A. and used by
permission.

Although unpublished previously, "Why Should People Care?" was first presented as
a lecture at an International Symposium on Human Rights, Retardation and Research.
Entitled "Choices on Our Conscience," the Symposium was held on October 16, 1971,
at the Shoreham Hotel in Washington, D.C., under the sponsorship of the Joseph P.
Kennedy, Jr. Foundation.

Grateful acknowledgement is made to Random House, Inc. for permission to quote
from the copyrighted works of Elie Wiesel.

Excerpts from THE ACCIDENT by Elie Wiesel, Translated from the French by Anne
Borchardt, © Editions du Seuil 1961. English translation © Elie Wiesel 1962. From
DAWN by Elie Wiesel, Translated from the French by Frances Frenaye, © Editions
du Seuil 1960, English translation © Elie Wiesel 1961. From NIGHT by Elie Wiesel,
Translated from the French by Stella Rodway, © Les Editions De Minuit, 1958.
English translation © Mac Gibbon & Kee, 1960. Reprinted with the permission of Hill
and Wang (now a division of Farrar, Straus & Giroux, Inc.).

Excerpts from *The Gates of the Forest* by Elie Wiesel. Translated by Frances Frenaye.
Copyright © 1966 by Holt, Rinehart and Winston. Excerpts from The Jews of Silence
by Elie Wiesel. Translated by Neal Kozodoy. Copyright © 1966 by Holt, Rinehart and
Winston. Excerpts from *Legends of Our Time* by Elie Wiesel. Translated by Steven
Donadio. Copyright © 1968 by Elie Wiesel. Excerpts from *The Town Beyond the Wall*
by Elie Wiesel. Translated by Stephen Becker. Copyright © 1964 by Elie Wiesel.
Reprinted by permission of Holt, Rinehart and Winston, Publishers.

Library of Congress Cataloging in Publication Data

Roth, John K
   A consuming fire.

   Bibliography: p.
   1. Holocaust, Jewish (1939–1945) 2. Wiesel, Elie,
1928– —Criticism and interpretation. 3. Holocaust
(Jewish Theology) I. Title.
D810.J4R667   940'.04'924   78–52442
ISBN 0–8042–0812–3

For
Richard
Fred
and
Elie

Out of love for mankind . . . I conceived it as my task to create difficulties everywhere. (Søren Kierkegaard, *Concluding Unscientific Postscript* [Princeton: Princeton University Press, 1974], p. 166)

Working in all sorts of different ways in different people, it is the same God who is working in all of them. (1 Cor. 12:6, The Jerusalem Bible)

Contents

Preface

Elie Wiesel. A Jewish storyteller who struggles with the Holocaust, the Nazi attempt to exterminate his people. He is the reason for this book. Accounting for that fact lies ahead; it need not occur here. But other items should be mentioned. For instance, premises and objectives that motivate this writing.

Why am I doing this? Anyone who studies the Holocaust ought to ask that question. Two responses, one general and the other more specific, clarify what this book is about. The first line of thought begins by saying: the Holocaust is interesting. Interesting? But in what ways and at what price? No doubt it is interesting that countless persons died and suffered, but isn't the Holocaust different from the Super Bowl or fine cooking? Isn't it something which, if kept only in the category of "interesting," is mocked or in turn mocks us?

Oh, but not just "interesting," goes a further rationale. People can learn from such study how to make the future better. The real motivation is to be warned by the past, to make sure that these things never happen again. This approach seems more satisfactory. At least it moves from an aesthetic category to something like an ethical outlook. But pause. Does history testify that the study of it improves things? Or is the truth closer to Hegel's view? History—including the study of history—is "the slaughter-bench at which the happiness of peoples, the wisdom of states, and the virtue of individuals have been sacrificed."[1] Learning can instill pessimism and despair as well as optimism and hope. When the slaughter of millions is focused, what result should one expect?

Still another option runs like this: "I am Jewish and I need to know what happened," or "I am not Jewish, but I need to know what happened." Again the ever-present "why?" Well, one might say, even if we can't guarantee that study will improve history, it still seems important to understand the persons and forces that produced Holocaust events. At least to understand how or why something occurred contains some justification of its own, and that understanding might help us, too.

Yes, it is possible to see patterns of action in the Holocaust events, to detect reasons why things went one way rather than another. Political, sociological, psychological, even philosophical and religious analyses can be made, and they do shed light for understanding. But what if the net result should still be that things don't yield an answer to "why"? Or, to put it another way, what if the accumulated answers leave us mainly with the impression that human circumstances are fundamentally beyond reason, not just absurd but all too destructively so? Then would "needing to know" be worthwhile, or would it drive us into a dark night of the soul where loss is just as likely as gain?

Other scenarios could be played. But one sound conclusion lives in the three already noted. The Holocaust reveals that the interesting can be horrible, that the ethical drive can point toward its own demise, that the search for understanding can turn on itself by uncovering events beyond comprehension. It does not follow, however, that it is better to ignore that portion of the past. In spite of, indeed because of, the fact that we live in a world shadowed by threats of mass destruction, it becomes imperative to take the gamble of Holocaust encounters. Reason? *By witnessing in retrospect the worst that has befallen humanity, by facing the disillusionment and despair that such an encounter must produce—perhaps only by doing those things—we may rediscover or locate for the first time resources of heart, mind, and will without which there will be too little checking of destruction in the future.*

A risky gamble? Of course. Too risky? Not when you consider alternatives. Ignorance is *not* bliss. What is not known *can and does* hurt us. Thinking that there are "unthinkable" possibilities—and therefore that we are somehow protected from the worst that men and women are capable of doing—probably people are never immune from that illusion. But efforts to forestall it are crucial for human well-being, and they will not be rooted strongly enough unless we face honestly the reality and aftermath of a Holocaust that leaves our own times charged with unprecedented destruction-potential.

Operating with that cluster of first assumptions, this book drives them deeper by exploring religious and theological implications of the Holocaust, particularly as they are illuminated by the writings of Elie Wiesel. Moreover, it explores those religious and theological implications in their bearing on Christianity, and even more sharply in their bearing on American versions of Christian life. As a Christian and as an American, I am convinced that profound encounters with God, mediated by the Holocaust as seen by Elie Wiesel, lie in store for any persons like me who will look. Thus I have written for any who will read, but with special concern for Christians in the United States.

Common Christian assumptions about God, Jesus, and the future are tested by the Holocaust at every turn—and often found wanting. My experience with Elie Wiesel, however, teaches me to discern provocative variations in ancient biblical texts and Christian themes. The result, I believe, can be much-needed Christian stances better able to withstand and move forward from the consuming fires of Auschwitz. Emphasis falls less on answers—Christian or any other—and more on ways of keeping questions in view, of struggling and coping with them. Jewishness like Elie Wiesel's understands that the fate of humanity depends on pursuing questions that we cannot, must not answer. In a post-Holocaust—or pre-Holocaust?—world, *Christians need to become more Jewish, Wiesel-style.*

But enough about premises and hints concerning their development. The full unfolding of their story is for chapters ahead. What remains to be said here are words of thanks. First, I am indebted to Irving Greenberg. His invitation to speak at a conference on "The Work of Elie Wiesel and the Holocaust Universe" (September 7–9, 1976) led me to project this book. Greenberg's writing has also influenced my own. For example, he says that "no statement, theological or otherwise, should be made that would not be credible in the presence of . . . burning children."[2] That principle puts every form of speech and silence under judgment. It finds all of them lacking. But if there are times and places where this book speaks well, that result is due to Irving Greenberg's criterion.

Other persons who deserve thanks include: Maynard Mack, Ron Jager, Sue Schall, and all of my colleagues at the National Humanities Institute, Yale University, where I did much of the writing as a Fellow during the 1976–77 academic year; Ben Beliak, Michael Berenbaum, Harry James Cargas, Thomas Idinopulos, and Moshe Lazar, all of whom gave timely advice; Richard A. Ray, Director of the John Knox Press, whose encouragement kept me moving ahead, and Joan Crawford, whose careful editing makes the reader's task so much easier. Finally, there are three men who have long been my guides in a

continuing search that might be called: How an American Christian
Is Deepening That Identity by Embracing Jewishness.

This book is dedicated to Richard L. Rubenstein, Frederick Sontag, and Elie Wiesel. In ways very different, Jewish spirit lives in each
of them, just as in ways very different they have been my teachers and
nourished my life. Each of these men stands to me not quite like a
father, but certainly like an elder brother—provoking, teasing, caring,
making me glad or angry but always in the right amount. All of them
make me write.

Since 1966 I have studied Richard Rubenstein's reflections on the
Holocaust. That effort repaid itself long before he became my
Humanities Institute colleague, but in the year that we shared together, talking about the Holocaust, discussing the Bible, meeting in
each other's offices, he became my good friend. I do not find all of his
conclusions congenial. His God is too impersonal; his thinking too
political and sociological. From time to time he will recognize himself
in these pages as my opposition. More frequently, I hope, he will find
the influence of his questions, his concern for honesty, his openness
to give every point of view its due. What this book says will not always
be to his liking, but hardly anything written here has gone to print
without my bringing it into contact with his thought.

Of the three, Frederick Sontag is closest to me. I was his college
student, and now we teach and write together. Family ties link us; we
share faith in common, too. Religiously, Fred cuts against the grain.
As a Christian, he tests that tradition, quizzes it philosophically, even
as he testifies to it. Nothing stays quite the same. For one thing, God
himself is cast in new light as One who is needlessly implicated in evil.
Not exactly the epitome of conventional Christianity, it must be ad-
mitted. But that option is intriguing, worth tracking down, in a world
of consuming fire. *Strange as it may seem, an encounter with a guilty
God may be what is needed to set human souls on fire for good.* For
almost twenty years Fred Sontag has had me pursuing myself by
seeking God, and seeking myself by pursuing God. His reward will
be in heaven. But for now, at least in part, this book may do.

Then there is Elie. There is also his wife, Marion, who makes it
possible for me to read his recent books with her sensitive English
translations. At his encouragement, I tried to write a book that is less
about him and more about life as I have found it thus far. I have

produced neither a biography, a literary analysis, nor even a philo-sophical critique of his writings, anymore than I have written a his-tory of Holocaust events. Instead I wanted to see what would result by weaving two strands together: my own Christian experience and my reading of the Holocaust via his books. This writer has changed my life, and my utmost thanks for his friendship must be that I try always to make that change a blessing. Thus, the outcome of my reflection is shared in the hope that it may assist others to venture in similar ways and to find new determination to thwart absurdity and indifference.

Elie Wiesel might be more comfortable if I had cut loose and said what was on my mind without concentrating on him so much. He is correct: if I have more to say about the Holocaust, God, and Christi-anity, it will need to move beyond the configuration found here. But for now Elie Wiesel had to have a central place. His story, his stories, are so crucial for our times, so lasting in their significance for the human future. They should make a difference to Christian life in America, and my aim is to help make them better known in that setting.

The best part of this book is the Prologue. Generously contributed by Wiesel himself, it poses a theme-question that holds the chapters together: why should people care? The tone and message of that essay are characteristic, with one exception: God is hardly mentioned. And yet God is not far behind the scenes, and Wiesel's question, unpacked in what follows, brings God to the fore. In doing so, it engages human lives all the more.

But how? To what ends? Such questions linger long after writing and reading are done. If they do so consciously, the writing will not be without reason, the reading not without point. And to the extent that such consciousness moves men, women, and children to choose life with compassion, steps are taken to make good the Psalmist's still problematic claim: "All thy works shall give thanks to thee, O LORD." (Ps. 145:10)

John K. Roth
Claremont, California
Advent 1977

A Prologue:
Why Should People Care?
by
Elie Wiesel

A disciple came to Rebbe Israel Baal Shem Tov for advice: many learned scholars claim to be Masters—how is one to distinguish between the authentic and the fake? When in doubt, said the Rebbe, ask them a certain question about the way to attain purity of thought; he who claims he has all the answers is a fake.

Since the same detection-device could also be used on novelists, I shall be quick to state that not only do I not possess all the answers —I don't even know all the questions.

I admit, though, that I do know some and the one before us is among them: whether people should or should not care, is surely one of the questions essential to men and women of my generation, and perhaps of all generations.

Had Adam shown more interest in the growth and welfare of his two sons, he might have saved one from becoming the first murderer and the other the first victim in history; but he was too busy with his own problems—such as women, ecology, knowledge, God—too busy with himself to care about other human beings. The first genocide was nothing if not the result of indifference.

In morality as in literature—or in any field of human creativity— indifference is the enemy; indifference to evil is worse than evil for it is sterile as well. This is true of both individuals and communities. The opposite of art is not hate but apathy. Revolutionary movements cease to be revolutionary when they cease to be movements. Submissiveness inevitably leads to decadence. If both the Catholic Church and the Communist closed-society go through unprecedented crises and upheavals, is it not because the younger generation resents the formal and self-centered faith of its parents? Had these parents cared more about society at large when they were young, humankind today would be less threatened by an anger it seems unable to contain, let alone control.

Examples? The history of my people is full of them. While count-less men and women were being crucified, Pontius Pilate refused to let his emotions interfere. Scores of communities were wiped out by Crusaders—yet their leaders are to this day revered as saints. Or, in more recent times: Jassy 1941. Hundreds, perhaps thousands of men, women, and children are being massacred in the streets. The atrocities perpetrated during the pogrom manage to outrage even the German authorities. People are literally butchered. Others are loaded onto freight-trains without food, water, or air; they lose their minds before they find their death. Though all had been honest citizens, good neighbors, and loyal business associates, they had not one friend in the Christian community—not one acquaintance—who felt it necessary to warn them. For several days most adult Christians had been aware of what was being planned—and not one cared enough to break the silence.

More examples? Transylvania 1944. Spring. A few weeks before Normandy. The war is virtually over. The Red Army has reached the nearby Carpathian mountains. There is not a single capital in the free world where the existence of death-factories is unknown. Yet—no one bothers to inform—much less help—six hundred thousand Jews whom Eichmann and his units are rounding up in towns like mine. Everybody knows—except the Jews. Everybody knows that Ausch-witz is more than a name—except the Jews who are destined to be shipped off to Auschwitz. Had they been warned, they might have escaped into the mountains surrounding my town.

The truth? Let's face it: the world didn't care, humanity was unconcerned. Jews were expendable. Hitler understood it. His deci-sion to implement his so-called Final Solution was not a sudden one. It was preceded by numerous plans, smaller in scope, designed to measure their impact on the free world. After each blow, he waited. Only when he realized that no one would do more than pay lip-service, did he give the Eichmanns the green light. And ten thousand human beings perished daily.

Hitler must have known that FDR had rejected the ridiculously modest pleas from Jewish leaders to bomb the railways leading to Auschwitz. The pretext: not a single bomb could be diverted from the overall war effort. While FDR justified his decision, Jews from more villages entered the kingdom of night.

Had Hitler been content with fulfilling his pledges relating to the Jewish question—in other words: had he stayed in Poland and exterminated its Jews, without invading Belgium and France, would the free powers have waged war against the Third Reich? In this limited respect, Hitler's intuition did not mislead him. As far as Jews were concerned, his hands were untied.

In a broader sense, Nazi ideology was built on the gruesome concept that people can be conditioned by and reduced to total apathy. In its land, as epitomized in Auschwitz, individual survival was linked to the loss of identity. Upon their arrival, the inmates were told to forget who they were—to forget parents and friends and comrades —and obey one single law: everyone was on his or her own. The slightest inclination toward selflessness was the surest and shortest way to death.

But, strange as it may seem, the experiment failed. We have learned from witnesses and Holocaust-chroniclers that those victims who maintained their identity and found enough strength in themselves to care for a fellow-prisoner had a better chance to survive both physically and morally. To stay alive, one had to save others from despairing. To preserve one's sanity, one had to help others resist madness. There was no other way.

Is this supposed to be the answer to the question why people should care? If so, it is an answer given *"en désespoir de cause."* The motivation is not pure enough for you? Sorry—I belong to a generation that asks little from people—and expects even less.

What do we—children of the Holocaust—have to offer? Our experience, our memory. The trouble is that we have lived beyond time and therefore find it difficult to distinguish between past and present. I remember what I see now; today's reality reflects yesterday's.

Did the war end in 1945? If so, why are so many youngsters falling week after week on battlefields all over the world? One war has ended but others, many others have replaced it. Political wars, religious wars, tribal wars: a bizarre combination of the middle ages and the nuclear era. Social conflicts, racial tensions, economic upheavals: our society has never been as divided, as torn from within. The vocabulary sounds familiar: ghettos, discrimination, hunger, gestapo-tactics, resistance, indifference, extermination. Haven't people learned anything? Haven't we made any step forward? We walk on the moon, but haven't managed to come closer to our neighbor or to ourselves; we try so hard to push back the horizon that we now live with no horizon at all. In conquering space, we forget our soul. We think our minds dominate matter, whereas they are dominated by it.

The war ended in 1945—but who won it? And are all its victims buried? What about those of today and tomorrow? How many of us display some awareness of the nuclear menace? We have become indifferent to our own death.

Our elders were indifferent a generation ago—and we were indifferent to the tragedies in Biafra and East-Pakistan. But indifference today is no longer a sin—it is punishment in itself. This planet may, at any moment, as a result of madness or stupidity, explode in the face of God—and we don't even think about it. We don't even care, we are not even concerned. The Messiah may come by accident, said a Hasidic Master, one hundred and fifty years ago. Today he would say: the end of the world may come by accident. How can it be saved? That's not for the novelist to say. There is a "Savior" for that particular purpose. But the Savior, according to the tradition of my people, is not one person; he is in all of us. Which means: we can—we must —help him help us. Which means: we must appeal to our collective memory: only the tale of what was done to my people can save humankind from a similar fate. Which means: we must care—lest we fall victims to our own indifference.

Could this be the answer? No. But—it is the question.

I
All Events Are Linked

He holds in his power the soul of every living thing, and the breath of each man's body. (Job 12:10, The Jerusalem Bible)

And if you are Christ's, then you are Abraham's offspring, heirs according to promise. (Gal. 3:29)

In Jewish history, all events are linked. (Elie Wiesel, *Messengers of God,* p. xiii)

Forethoughts: Pieces in Search of Puzzles

Remember the Prologue. Otherwise nothing that follows will make much sense. For this book plays variations on Elie Wiesel's opening theme: Why Should People Care? It begins with fragments and then tries to work a puzzle of moods ranging from despair and anger to encouragement, expectation, and hope. Why—how and for what—should people care? Parts of a response include . . .

A BIBLICAL WARNING: " 'Take care therefore not to forget the covenant which Yahweh your God has made with you, by making a carved image of anything that Yahweh your God has forbidden you; for Yahweh your God is a consuming fire, a jealous God.' " (Deut. 4:23–24, The Jerusalem Bible)

A NEW TESTAMENT PROMISE: "We have been given possession of an unshakeable kingdom. Let us therefore hold on to the grace that we have been given and use it to worship God in the way that he finds acceptable, in reverence and fear. For our *God* is a *consuming fire.*" (Heb. 12:28–29, The Jerusalem Bible)

A PARABLE ABOUT REBBE MENAHEM-MENDL OF KOTZK: "The Midrash tells the episode of the traveler who loses his way in the forest. He sees a castle in flames. It's an empty castle, thinks the traveler. Suddenly he hears a voice crying: 'Help, help me, I am the owner of the castle!' And the Rebbe repeats: 'The castle is ablaze, the forest is burning, and the owner cries for help; what does it mean? That the castle is not empty and that there is an owner!'

"And the Rebbe began to tremble and all those present trembled with him." (Elie Wiesel, *Souls on Fire,* pp. 250–251)

A TALE: A reader once encountered three pieces of writing. They were different, and yet they shared themes and concepts. More importantly, they sent sparks flying in his thoughts and feelings. Connections between the fragments were far from clear, but the reader knew that fire drew them together. Because he had been thinking for a long time about an event now called the Holocaust, he linked the three passages and began to write a book.

The goal? To find out what the fragments mean. To identify better the owners of castles, to be moved more effectively by their cries for help in the midst of burning. To encounter the consuming fire which is God. To discover why he wrote this tale, to see if it . . . no, if *he* can measure up to Elie Wiesel's challenge: "Every writer today, no matter who, Jewish or not Jewish—but particularly Jewish—must write with the Holocaust as background, as criteria."[1]

Did he succeed? Yes and no. His life continued, apparently not much different than before. Of some things, though, he is being persuaded. For one: every writer today, no matter who, Christian or not Christian—*but particularly Christian*—must write with the Holocaust as background, as criteria. For another: Camus is correct when he says that "man is not entirely to blame; it was not he who started history; nor is he entirely innocent, since he continues it."[2] And because Camus is correct it is well to supplement that statement: (1) God is not entirely to blame; he gives human life its freedom; nor is he entirely innocent since freedom's possibilities and boundaries are in his hands. (2) Jesus is not entirely to blame; he suffered and died to save people from themselves; nor is he entirely innocent since his love desires and expects more than men and women give and thus permits countless, unnecessary crucifixions every day—their waste reduced, but not eliminated, if people can sense his suffering with them.

This reader/author works to comprehend that the point of those persuasions is less to fix guilt and more to convert life so that causes for blame are reduced. Not least by struggling with himself, he is discovering that the importance of such conversion is no less than its difficulty.

A FACT: From 1933 to 1945 the German state under Adolf Hitler attempted to rid Europe—if not the world—of Jews. Six million perished.

A QUANDARY: Was that act unprecedented in human history, and is it also unrepeatable? Opinions clash. . . . People have always killed. Greed, racism, religious bigotry, and even genocide left a bloody trail long before swastikas and Stars of David walked the same streets. . . . No, this time the quantity and kind of killing combined to yield something new. In this case the killing was genocide carried out— self-consciously and conscientiously—in accord with an ideology in which the elimination of Jews was not only the means to racial- national purity but also an end in itself. No matter if history exhibits other instances to fit that pattern. Advances in the technology of death, administrative apparatus, communications networks, transpor- tation, all of these gave people killing tools that earlier generations lacked. Thus, never before was it possible to make genocide a system- atic, assembly-line operation, one which obtained the cooperation of every sector of the society, including countless decent and cultured people and even many of the victims themselves. Never before was murder routinized on so large a scale; never before was evil so banal. . . . Well even so, it can't or won't happen again. History doesn't repeat. Besides, we've learned better. . . . Maybe history doesn't repeat exactly, but don't people have a way of making precedents out of almost anything, including the unprecedented?

A CONCEPT AND A NAME: Holocaust—a great or total destruction by fire (from the Greek *holokaustos,* burnt whole). Thus goes one dictionary entry. To speak of "the Holocaust" is to say much more. That designation is hardly neutral, at least not if one wonders: what's in a name?

Names do not appear out of thin air. They are chosen and be- stowed. In this situation, Jews themselves did the naming, and the heritage of that act is significant. The roots are partly biblical. In the

Septuagint, a Greek translation of Jewish scripture dating from the third century B.C., *holokauston* is used for the Hebrew *olah,* which means "literally 'what is brought up.' " Passages in which the original Hebrew reads *olah* are usually "rendered in English as 'an offering made by fire unto the Lord,' 'burnt offering,' or 'whole burnt offering.' "[3]

The Jerusalem Bible uses "holocaust" in its translations. For examples see: 1 Samuel 15:22; Psalms 40:6–7 and 50:7–9; Isaiah 1:11; Jeremiah 6:20, 7:21, 14:12; Hosea 6:5–6; Amos 5:21–22; and Micah 6:6. See also Mark 12:32–34 and Hebrews 10:6. The story of the sacrifice of Isaac in Genesis 22 is crucial in this regard as well.

Most of the biblical passages just mentioned portray God as desiring justice, mercy, and faithfulness to laws written in the heart—not the burnt sacrifice of animal flesh offered in religious ritual. What one finds in the Holocaust, however, is that all too often justice, mercy, and faithfulness were themselves engulfed by a consuming fire. Not without reason, then, a Hebrew term for "the Holocaust" is *Shoah,* meaning "catastrophe."

Not everyone, certainly not every Jew, identifies with attempts to invest the destruction of European Jewry with special religious significance, let alone to maintain specific interpretations that Jewish victims are rightly viewed as self-sacrifices for the Sanctification of God's Name *(Kiddush Hashem).* For many persons, the Holocaust-as-Shoah, as catastrophe, says more than enough. And yet that second way of naming is difficult to separate from the first.

The Holocaust: Either way . . . both ways . . . the name fits. Reason? It lends itself—straightforwardly, ironically, tragically—to so many experiences and feelings.

However one reads the event, there were burnings and sacrifices, millions of them whole and total. There were offerings to gods as well as to the Lord. The name conveys lamentation and rage. It can signify continuity with a long history of Jewish persecution, or it can identify a rupture, an unbridgeable chasm between a world gone forever and one that is too much with us. Faith and its loss, hope and its impossibility, love and its despair—all of these realities and more are contained in "the Holocaust."

But isn't it unfortunate, says one voice of cool objectivity, that such a volatile concept got attached to this sad occurrence? To speak of the Holocaust—doesn't that distort fact with emotion and keep passion inflamed to an extent that is psychologically explosive and politically unfeasible?

What to reply? Maybe nothing. Silence might be best. Maybe with the observation that you can't please everyone. Maybe with the reminder that cool objectivity can be a killer, too. Maybe with recognition that names are not indifferent, that they can indeed keep men and women in the breach, but that as it was once given to Adam to name every living creature, so it is given to us to assume responsibility for naming *events*—not only so nothing important is hidden, but so we alert ourselves to the sanctity of life itself.

What's in a Name: The Holocaust? Adam did not have the burden of answering that particular question. But we do . . . and God does, too.

A PROTEST: "There is a legend in the Midrash that disturbs me. When did God decide to liberate his people from Egyptian bondage? When Pharaoh ordered that living Jewish children be used as bricks for his pyramids, the Angel Michael caught one such child and brought it before God. And when God saw the child—already disfigured—He was overcome by compassion and love and chose to redeem his people.

"And often I say to myself: *Ribono shel olam,* Master of the universe, one child was enough to move you—and one million children were not?"[4] (Elie Wiesel, "Art and Culture After the Holocaust")

A POSSIBILITY: " 'Is there a man among you who would hand his son a stone when he asked for bread? Or would hand him a snake when he asked for a fish? If you, then, who are evil, know how to give your children what is good, how much more will your Father in heaven give good things to those who ask him!' " (Jesus of Nazareth in Matt. 7:9–11, The Jerusalem Bible)

AN APPRAISAL: "And God saw everything that he had made, and behold, it was very good. And there was evening and there was morning, a sixth day." (Gen. 1:31)

A TEST: How was it on the eighth day? What did God see in 1934 and in 1944, and how did he find creation then? How do we find it as we look back? Shall life unfold today and tomorrow so that men, women, and children everywhere (and even God himself) can better cry out their versions of the psalm—"O taste and see that the LORD is good! Happy is the man who takes refuge in him!" (Ps. 34:8)—with tears of joy that drown pain and sorrow?

A TRIAL: If God is not put to the test with impunity, neither are human lives. Everywhere, all of us—God included—must be challenging each other: *what is going on here?*

How Can I Explain Its Hold on Me?

Something puzzles me. It has for a long time. I don't regard myself as an emotional person. Even-tempered, quiet, few uncontrolled moments of ecstasy or depression—that's me. So why do I sometimes find myself about to cry? Nobody notices, but why do my eyes well up with tears in church on Sunday mornings?

People go to church for many reasons. One of mine is to feel tears. Fortunately, we are beyond an arid respectability that deemed it irrational, unscientific—in a word, inappropriate—to speak openly about religious experience. Emotion also has regained a rightful place in spiritual life, and I feel that my tears are an emotional expression with religious significance. True, no aspect of self-appraisal is more liable to deception than interpreting one's own emotions. A perspective unfolds nonetheless. It struggles to life because of, even in spite of, Elie Wiesel, the man who makes this book possible and necessary.

His experience is the only justification for my attempting to intrude into yours. But that justification is sufficient. Join in. Become a pilgrim with the two of us, and you shall discover, unwillingly perhaps, that all events are linked. Every one traces forward or backward to times and places that disarray. My tears and now your reading eyes are linked with Elie Wiesel's life and thought. Even if you had never scanned these pages, or even if you go no further, that connection still exists. It has a hold on all of us.

Better to examine that fact than to ignore it—such is the justifying premise for urging you along. Too vague a promise, too uninteresting? Very well, my failure and your . . . no, *our* loss. For it is neither immodesty nor overstatement to say that the issues at stake here embrace "the soul of every living thing, and the breath of each man's body." Conscious responses to them—or the lack thereof—determine the fate of humanity and history . . . and, yes, the fate of God, too.

A recent *Who's Who in America* condenses Elie Wiesel to twenty lines. They outline a common pattern of success in these United States. The sketch notes that Wiesel was born in Sighet, Rumania on September 30, 1928, to Shlomo and Sarah Feig Wiesel. It tells that he studied in Paris at the Sorbonne from 1947 to 1950, and that he traveled to the United States in 1956, where he became a naturalized citizen in 1963. Numerous books authored by Wiesel are listed, along with the fact that he holds several honorary degrees. Mention is also made of his distinguished professorship, his marriage, and his winning of prominent literary prizes. Ironically, however, *Who's Who* is silent about the very fact that accounts for its entry about him. A final line should read: Jewish survivor of Auschwitz.

The Holocaust—that event-symbol of destruction binds us all. It defies rationality, even as we learn more about it and discover that it once had an understandable logic, indeed one so irresistible as to transform the world. It mocks morality, not only because innocent people were slaughtered and the guilty too often did not come to justice, but also because for the most part the people who carried out or permitted the orders were ordinary, decent, good people much like you and me. The Holocaust also undermines optimism about humanity and faith in God, not least because we now understand that without hopes for God and trust in him, this particular configuration of history could not have been.

Lists of disillusionment can be multiplied times over. They become so overwhelming that we may yet try to live as though the past was never present. Unsettling though the fact may be, that option is not fully possible: too many men and women are committed to breaking silence, to keeping memory pained and keen. "Those who cannot remember the past," warns a plaque at Dachau, "are condemned to repeat it."[5] Holocaust witnesses and prophets work to forestall human undoing, but can that hope outweigh the fear that people learn too-little-too-late, or nothing at all?

"In truth," states Elie Wiesel, "I think I have never spoken about the Holocaust except in one book, *Night,*—the very first—where I tried to tell a tale directly, as though face to face with the experience."[6] Correct . . . but only to a degree. Wiesel has stated, *"Night* was the foundation; all the rest is commentary."[7] All events are linked, and thus Wiesel's writings are rarely more than once-removed from the flames and smoke of Auschwitz. Indeed his continuing accomplishment is that of having the courage to remember and interrogate the Holocaust—forecast, real, and aftermath—in ways that honor the victims and teach the living.

This man does not see himself primarily as a philosopher, theologian, or political theorist. Instead he is a storyteller. Storytellers can explore questions without answering them straight out, and that possibility attracts Wiesel as a way of confronting what can now be called a Holocaust Universe. Its reality and significance elude words, at least those that are direct. Thus, the prospects afforded by theory-building disciplines seem less fruitful to Wiesel than those offered by the indirect approach of telling tales. And yet, in the midst of recounting stories linked to—if not of—the Holocaust, philosophy, theology, politics come to life in ways that theory alone never yields.

Writing mainly in French, Wiesel employs varied forms of prose and poetry, fact and fiction, as he draws heavily on Jewish legend and tradition. Echoes of modern thinkers such as Kierkegaard, Kafka, Buber, and Camus can be heard in his writings, too. He is transforming all of these resources into a literature of lasting power and moral authority. In spite of and at the same time because of this success, the gift of Elie Wiesel—born in suffering and silence—remains mysterious. Perhaps more than anyone, he is troubled by the meanings of his own survival and achievement, and by the duties that both lay upon him: "Man is responsible not only for what he says, but also for what he does not say."[8]

Return for a moment to my tears. Crucial to underscore that they come neither in every place nor at my command: they overtake me. The tune of a hymn, a passage of scripture, a memory flash evoked by a sermon, even silent waiting—any of these may tighten muscles in my throat and blur my eyes. But if I expect or think about tears, they do not come, and thus I wonder if my writing will end them altogether. Arising almost exclusively in settings of Christian worship, I know that they are related to the Holocaust as I have seen it through-and-in the eyes of Elie Wiesel. But the feelings I must penetrate are not found mainly in reading about that event, not in teaching about it, and not as I follow the typewriter keys that form the words on this page.

What messages do I hear and what acts do I perform in church? Interpretation-clues may live there. Prominent messages are these: The world's existence is not a chance occurrence but God's creation. Human life is not absurd; it has meaning and purpose underwritten by God himself. Jesus is the Christ, the Son and Messiah of God, revealing that God's nature is love, that sin—individual and corporate —is not only judged but can also be forgiven, that death is overcome in resurrection, and that the goodness of God prevails over evil.

Communicating and responding to those messages, the acts performed include: thanksgiving, singing, and celebration for life and good news; confession of faith that God is our Father and that Jesus is Lord; acknowledgment of sin, of failure to love God and to serve one's neighbor; assurance of pardon so that one is encouraged to try again; the bringing of gifts; listening for God's direction in scripture, sermon, and prayer; asking God to heal the world's pain by making men and women instruments of his peace; sometimes sacraments such as baptism and the Lord's Supper, which nourish a community of faith and hope; always the injunction that Christians come together for preparation to meet the persons, places, problems, and possibilities of a new week with courage and strength to do God's good will.

How sharp the contrast between messages and actions that I experience for an hour each Sunday and those of the other hours that form any of history's weeks. Having encountered Holocaust history and the writings of Elie Wiesel, that difference is reason enough to cry. What the future may hold I don't know, but at this point I am reasonably sure that I will continue to profess my Christian faith by worship on Sunday mornings. To stop would be to cancel the journey I am on, and that adventure is too compelling. Sunday morning gives hope, desire, and even faith about good things that could, should, and perhaps shall be. The Holocaust reveals a pit, foreshadowed by centuries, that may have swallowed God's love and humanity's hope, or at least may have provided a prelude for events that will. The quest is to see what is going on here.

My tears are many things: despair and expectation, fear and courage, anger and love. They include rebellion and incomprehension; submission, thanksgiving, and understanding are also present. These emotions are linked. To start with one is to be carried through them all, even to feel them all at once. The difficulties of sorting them out, of interpreting them, become all the more complex when I recognize that they have multiple objects, too. States, churches, persons, some known to me first-hand, others from times before my own—those are some of the targets.

Three stand out. Beyond myself, Elie Wiesel and God are the other two. I knew about the Holocaust before I read Wiesel, but he makes the event burn inside me. And God . . . unseen and perhaps unreal (though my faith, strangely nourished by the Holocaust, says something different) . . . encounters with God are at the heart of the matter. I find that the Holocaust, as event-and-symbol, offers itself as a revelation. Not that some specific message of God's is communicated. Not that the event discloses some unmistakable action of God within history. Rather the Holocaust is a revelation insofar as it lays bare the need to explore my Christian faith from the roots on up. These problems could be my hang-ups alone. Nobody else needs to care. But those convictions are not mine. Otherwise I wouldn't bother with this writing.

Add one more pivotal figure to this dialogue: you. Should you be Christian, please inquire with me. We can seek our way together. Should you be Jewish, you may simply wonder curiously what an American Protestant discovers as he explores Holocaust history, and then you may find that new steps can be taken to further understanding and honesty. Should you place yourself elsewhere in terms of creed or ethnic background, then bounce your moods and feelings off of mine and see whether our differences still leave us linked on common ground. And even if your conviction should be that "God-talk" is beside the point or out of the question, especially where the Holocaust is concerned, I would still urge you to spend a few hours with us. Not so your conviction will be changed, for life after Auschwitz may well be more troublesome with God than without, but so you will draw out what you would say instead. For of this much I am convinced: if we do not confront and share hopes and fears, despair and dreams, in the light of the Holocaust, our silence and blindness will leave us more vulnerable to some version of its repetition in the future. So whoever you may be, identify yourself as you go and link yourself to Elie Wiesel and me . . . and if you can, to God as well.

In his novel, *The Oath,* Elie Wiesel tells the story of Kolvillàg, a town that disappeared. We shall return to that place later. For now, only one line is important. As the old narrator begins to tell his tale to his young listener, a man who has experienced none of the story's events first-hand, the latter finds himself gripped by the story and the storyteller . . . puzzled, too. *"How can I explain its hold on me?"* he asks himself and thereby the reader as well (p. 16).[9] Already we have shared that question. Some pieces of the puzzle seem to be finding each other. Shall we hunt and find some more?

Compelled to Do the Same

In another vignette from *The Oath,* Azriel, the old storyteller, relates the tale of Kolvillàg to his young listener for a purpose. His aim? To quicken emotional tensions and links of the sort we have noted already; to bring to life a person whose existence is too much lacking in urgency, compassion, courage and too much inclined toward emptiness, feelings of insignificance, moods of futility spawned by life's terror and incomprehensibility. Azriel's plan? "Yes, that is the best method; it has been tested and proved. I'll transmit my experience to him and he, in turn, will be compelled to do the same. He in turn will become a messenger. And once a messenger, he has no alternative. He must stay alive until he has transmitted his message." (P. 33) Redeem lives, forestall tendencies to waste ourselves, encourage people to touch each other with care and respect instead of violence . . . by telling stories, by trying to turn men and women into messengers? Fantastic . . . and yet what is there to lose? More than we might surmise, for stories are not harmless and they are not told with impunity. Stories can kill life as well as give it. Elie Wiesel knows that he plays with fire.

There are no messengers without messages. So the question becomes: what is the message that should be lived, signed, sealed, delivered? No wholesale answers are possible. Each person finds and forms his own or there is none at all. Other persons can be the occasion; indeed they are indispensable for giving us stories to relate. But to repeat what someone else has given, without taking it and making it one's own, that is to be and to offer an empty husk.

Storytelling is a fickle business. You can intend to communicate something in giving a story, but stories also have lives of their own. They defy the boundaries of author—or communicator—intention, even as there is little control over their fate in a listener-reader's ears, eyes, and mind. What, if anything, will be changed or passed on? Those issues can loosen human ties just as they keep people joined together.

Elie Wiesel's stories invite people to become messengers. They are insistent. But this process is not something instantaneous that occurs as words are absorbed from his lips or from the pages of his books. The words have to do more than scratch the surface; they have to impel one inside in a search to locate where, how, and why an encounter with this man and his thought has occurred. Locate yourself in such a search by telling your own story of our meeting as I describe some links between Elie Wiesel and myself, links that leave me convinced that I have somehow been assigned to be a messenger. But if you choose to follow, be careful. You also may be commissioned.

The story of our meeting, Elie Wiesel, me, . . . and you, starts in Genesis. But we must cut centuries short and settle for only a few of time's fragments. Begin in September 1928. On the last day of that month (in that particular year the Jewish holiday of Simhat Torah, which celebrates the yearly completion-and-beginning of reading from the Law), Elie Wiesel was born. His name, Eliezer, was his grandfather's. God is in it, too; in Hebrew "El" refers to God. The name also traces back to a servant of Abraham and to a son of Moses: the former Abraham's heir until Isaac was born to him in old age; the latter so named because " 'The God of my father was my help, and delivered me from the sword of Pharaoh.' " (Exod. 18:4)

The family numbered six. Wiesel's father, who operated a grocery store, was a Jewish leader in Sighet. Before the Holocaust he had already experienced governmental persecution: jail and torture. At his insistence Wiesel pursued contemporary subjects—psychology, astronomy, modern Hebrew—and these studies were blended with his mother's concern that he receive traditional Jewish instruction in Torah, Talmud, and even the mysticism of Kabbalistic lore and Hasidic tales. Had events permitted, he might have fulfilled his mother's dream that he become both a Ph.D. and a rabbi . . . and you and I would never have heard his name.

None of that was to be. Scholar, teacher, writer—he would become all of these, though hardly in the typical sense or by the standard routes. And the intuition of his mother's counselor would also hold good: " ' "Sarah, daughter of David," . . . "I want you to know that one day your son will grow up to be a great man in Israel but neither you nor I will be alive to see it." ' "[10] Wiesel's older sisters, Hilda and Beatrice, survived the concentration camps and eventually were re-united with their brother. Auschwitz claimed his mother, father, and little sister, Tzipora.

Elie Wiesel has said that "there is no accident in life; there are only encounters."[11] If so, it is worth noting that in September 1928, I did not exist but my parents did. Miles to the west of Sighet—across a Europe still ravaged by the World War, hopeful, but not really, about democracy in the Germany of the Weimar Republic, skittish about economic inflation and instability—my mother and father lived in Louisville, Kentucky. A heartland city: segregated in a United States made isolationist by World War I; disillusioned about making the world safe for democracy; still optimistic about "the American way," even though economic crashes soon forthcoming would forge hard links across the Atlantic. Unknown and unexpected, although not altogether, the worlds of Hitler and Mussolini, Chamberlain and Churchill, Stalin and Roosevelt, were forming, converging to yield death camps and atomic explosions.

Blood in my father's line was Protestant Christian and German, in that order. Pacifists by religious conviction, his ancestors fled mili-tary conscription, emigrated from Europe in the first half of the nineteenth century, and found farm homes in northeastern Indiana. My mother grew up in similar surroundings. Her family went back to Scotch-Irish and German-Mennonite immigrants. Quaker ways were the main religious influence in her home. My father was at-tracted to the Presbyterian Church, and feeling called into the minis-try, he and his wife settled in Louisville so he could attend the Presby-terian seminary there.

In September 1940, while my father served a congregation in Grand Haven, Michigan, my parents had their second child. To the German Roth was added John King in honor of my mother's father, but also with an eye to scripture: "There was a man sent from God, whose name was John. He came for testimony, to bear witness to the light, that all might believe through him. He was not the light, but came to bear witness to the light." (John 1:6–8) Like stories, names are neither given nor received free of charge. It has not been my fate to become some latter-day John the Baptist or even a minister. But I reflect on that name-giving as I think about the contents of this book late on a gray winter afternoon.

It would be more than a year before full American involvement, but by September 1940, much of the world was burning. Only a year after Hitler's armies invaded Poland, Nazi flags flew over Denmark, Holland, Belgium, most of France, and Norway. The Allies had barely averted disaster with the Dunkirk evacuation. Cooperative agreements between Berlin, Rome, and Tokyo had been formalized. Later in that same year, Slovakia and Hungary (now including Sighet and portions of Transylvania, which Germany forced Rumania to cede to Hungary) would come under Nazi domination. Beliefs, hopes, lives were being shattered everywhere, but the world contained no war for me. Elie Wiesel's life was different. And yet not altogether.

Concerning the early war years, Wiesel remarks that "I don't remember too much; I didn't even suffer too much. I was too absorbed in my own studies. I was more aware about what went on three thousand years ago than what was going on in the present."[12] Months of second-class status went by. Then it was 1944. The war had already turned against the Nazis; their direct occupation of Hungary occurred because of the westward advances of Russian troops and crumbling Hungarian support for the Nazi cause. By April 4, 1945, no German forces would remain in Hungary, but their year-long presence proved fateful enough. Under the direction of Adolf Eichmann, Hungarian Jews (the Wiesels among them) were ghettoized, deported, gassed. Half a million disappeared.

Liberated by Americans on April 11, 1945, Elie Wiesel survives as a witness. Included in his story? After-the-fact astonishment and anger that the Jews of Sighet—partly through their own failure and partly through the indifference of others—were taken so late in the day and so unaware of Holocaust realities. And what of me—and you —in 1944–45 when Elie Wiesel worked and starved, suffered and survived, his way through Auschwitz and Buchenwald? I remember my mother's ration books, and I recall radio announcements of the bombings at Hiroshima and Nagasaki. Nothing more first-hand.

By the late 1950s it was a different world. Japan and Germany (at least in the West) were largely rebuilt, even prospering. Israel had struggled successfully to become an independent state. Communism was the threat perceived by most Americans, although a more immediate crisis over discrimination against blacks and other racial minorities was in the offing. Now in California, I entered Pomona College still only dimly aware of the implications of World War II for Jews and Christians alike, anticipating that I would follow my father's path and become a Presbyterian minister. Encounters with philosophy and theology, plus a growing love for a college environment as a place to live and work, would lead me toward a professorship instead of a pulpit, but not without the feeling that teaching is a form of ministry, too.

Meanwhile Elie Wiesel was at work, beginning to pour out images, words, and silences that now touch my life every day. The course that was bringing us toward encounter was mostly smooth and successful for me: education, marriage, job, children, teaching, and writing—all of these turned out well, with few crises and relatively little suffering. A good, not untypical, American life . . . enough advantage, accomplishment, and upward mobility to fuel native optimism and to keep hope high . . . experiences to leave faith born in youth not unchanged but more continuous than broken.

And how was it for him? In some ways, Wiesel's life far exceeds mine as an American success story. Distinguished as a professor, acclaimed and rewarded as a writer and lecturer, well-addressed at Central Park West, New York City—leaving out some details it sounds like an American dream come true. But the details are the tale. Post-liberation residence in France as a "stateless" refugee. Study of philosophy in Paris. A scramble to make ends meet. Travels to South America, Israel, and India as a reporter for an Israeli newspaper. Injury and hospitalization in New York after being struck by a taxi while on journalistic assignment at the United Nations. Citizenship in the United States almost by chance, as a solution to bureaucratic problems caused when his injury prevented him from returning to France to renew expired papers. And all the while haunted by visions of a past both gone and present, visions which put a double responsibility upon him: to write so that nothing essential is forgotten; to be silent so ideas and feelings mature and sift, so nothing is falsified, so the past may be transcended. Finally books . . . nearly twenty since his French-Catholic friend, François Mauriac, helped him find a publisher for *La Nuit (Night)* in 1958.

In the late sixties and early seventies, Elie Wiesel's life continued to unfold in writing and teaching. He also married and had a son. My life went likewise. Intellectual pursuits focused on the relations between God and evil, with some special Holocaust interests emerging. My wife and I had a son. I began to notice tears in church. Still, as late as 1971, I did not know that Elie Wiesel existed. Then in 1972 a friend suggested that I would find Wiesel's writings instructive. Quite by chance, I think, and certainly without knowing what awaited me, I bought some of his books and started to read them a few days after my second child, Sarah, was born on July 4th of that year. Circumstances, emotions, and words conspired to make this reading experience the most intense of my life. In two weeks I read all of Wiesel's books and was deeply moved. I felt compelled to respond in writing—to thank him, to clarify moods that he produced in me, to pursue a conversation, often one-way and ever perplexing, with God.

Even though three years elapsed before I met Wiesel face to face, he seemed somehow with me, and he became my invisible, but ever-present guide when my family and I went to live in Europe in 1973–74. Flying from New York to Milan, a Jew prepares for morning prayers somewhere over freezing Alps. I think of Jewish prayers, recounted by Wiesel, rising out of flaming pogroms from Kiev to Mainz. Days preceding Passover, Good Friday, and Easter . . . Red Square, Moscow . . . am I seeing any of Wiesel's "Jews of Silence," persecuted generations who yet remain faithful? September 1973 . . . Vienna . . . Arab terrorists and Jewish refugees. What should be done? Europe and the rest of the world (including the Jews) are still puzzled "one generation after." The village of Mörbisch on the Austro-Hungarian border . . . a look through "no man's land" and past guard towers. Out there, somewhere, is Sighet, where this odyssey began. Paris . . . the Sorbonne . . . what did Wiesel learn here? How to write? Perhaps. How to live with purpose when you are not sure that you want to live at all? Probably. Munich . . . Dachau . . . Elie Wiesel was never here. But of course he was and is. My trip there is a pilgrimage to meet him. I want to confront the task he is assigning.

Images, words, books—and always, always, questions—flow from his mind. I am drawn ever more into his Holocaust world. How

. . . by choice or compulsion? Some of both, I'm sure. And for what motives and reasons? That one is harder to answer. Sheer fascination with the history and drama of the Holocaust events. A feeling that it is important to communicate them in the hope that doing so will help to secure a future worth having. But if that were all, Elie Wiesel would not loom so large. There are better historians and political analysts, and often Wiesel's writings do touch the Holocaust only obliquely.

The dimension that grips me most is not the historical or the political, though it is rooted firmly in them. I am moved by Elie Wiesel because he pursues a conversation, often one-way and ever perplexing, with God before and after Auschwitz. He seeks to locate himself as Jew in that context. As Christian and American, I must try to do the same—not least because the blessings of my own life stand in such contrast to the fate of millions.

So far removed from each other by background, experience, and need, yet I feel linked to Elie Wiesel. And you . . . having come this far, you are also invited to become a witness, a messenger in the same spirit of service for the suffering and forsaken—and prodding for the comfortable and privileged—that motivates his writing. If you are moved, you will help us to accomplish our task and yours as well. And then though not compelled, God may do the same, remembering this promise to his people: " 'I will not leave you desolate; I will come to you.' " (John 14:18)

II
For the Moment
We Are All Survivors

Hear this, you aged men,
    give ear, all inhabitants of the land!
Has such a thing happened in your days,
    or in the days of your fathers?
Tell your children of it,
    and let your children tell their children,
    and their children another generation. (Joel 1:2–3)

All this happened to them as a warning, and it was
written down to be a lesson for us who are living at the
end of the age. The man who thinks he is safe must be
careful that he does not fall. (1 Cor. 10:11–12,
The Jerusalem Bible)

Thus, as one who has tried for some twenty-five years to
speak on the subject, I feel I must confess to a sense of
defeat. The witness was not heard. The world is world—
our testimony has made no difference. (Elie Wiesel, "Art
and Culture After the Holocaust" in *Auschwitz: Beginning
of a New Era?*, p. 405)

Not Peace, But a Sword

Words in this chapter's title appeared first in another book. They
were written in the chronicle of a community about to be destroyed
by hatred, racism, religious bigotry, greed, and every other rending
passion known to humanity and God (*The Oath,* p. 229). Such destruction history has repeated countless times. And in varied forms,
some far more painful than others, our common fate today is that for
the moment we are survivors all.

A precarious fate. How long we shall hold survivor-status may be
known to God, but for us the unfolding new has ways of its own. In
a moment, in the twinkling of an eye, we can all be changed, and it

remains a question to be answered by faith whether the dead shall be raised (1 Cor. 15:51–52). For the moment, though, we are survivors . . . of many things: diseases of body and spirit, natural disasters, political and economic upheavals, war, the Holocaust.

There are volumes of Holocaust history. They continue to roll off the presses in many languages.[1] Except for telling the story of my own meditation on this event, I have nothing to add to that record. Indeed it already defies any single human mind to come to terms with all the research done to date, let alone to digest it successfully as background for an inquiry such as this one. Nevertheless, to move along with Elie Wiesel some overview of the crucial period—1933–1945—is essential. Not only does that era involve a quality and magnitude of devastation rarely witnessed in human history. Those years also include human tendencies so common as to make plain that folly reigns whenever people assume that "it cannot happen again."

Events do not undo themselves; they stay what they are. The same is not true for interpretation of them. However dispassionate and "value-free" historical scholarship may claim to be, it remains a swirl of controversy aimed at defending this-or-that, refuting this-or-that, with living interests at stake. Nowhere is this reality more apparent than in studies of the Holocaust, for claims of collaboration and resistance, guilt and innocence, delusion and insight, clash with emotional impact whenever the subject is broached.[2] Since so much life and death are at stake—including our own senses of identity, which depend on historical views much more than we sometimes realize— this outcome is natural. Indeed that result is as it should be, provided new rounds of bitterness are not set loose by insistence that one view corners truth to the exclusion of every other.

In spite of and at the same time because of controversy there is consensus on numerous facts.[3] Six million Jews died at the hands of the Nazis. That estimate is the best known and most widely accepted piece of information about the Holocaust. As a general figure, it stands up well. Scholarly debates about numbers more precise are still in the same ballpark. Other data holds firm, too. Of the total Jewish population (around nine million persons) in pre-war Europe and the Soviet Union, about 70% perished in the Holocaust. The vast majority of victims were from Eastern Europe; over half from Poland, where the Nazi extermination effort was 90% successful. Judgments vary, but even conservative calculations suggest that at Auschwitz alone (located in Poland and largest of the killing centers), over one million Jews were gassed.[4] More statistics—endless—could be piled up. But what of the forces that produced them?

In March 1933, Heinrich Himmler established the first concentration camp in Nazi Germany.[5] It was situated near Munich at the town of Dachau. Part of a broad plan which included book-burnings, control of education, and state domination of cultural expression, Dachau did not serve merely to get criminals off the streets. The goal was to silence all dissent against the Nazi regime and to purge the Nazi party of factionalism. Thus, numerous Communists and clergymen, plus a large contingent of Jehovah's Witnesses, were thrown together with other "undesirables."

Although far removed from the Auschwitz of 1943, the Dachau of 1933 also contained Jews. They, too, were seen as threats but with a difference. Racism and anti-Semitism were at the heart of the matter, and the shock waves they produced are still with us. Their force started to build toward a crescendo on January 30, 1933, when Hitler took the Chancellor's oath from Paul von Hindenberg, President of the Weimar Republic.

As the works of Brecht, Klee, Kandinsky, and the Bauhaus movement make clear, Weimar Germany provided a lively environment for the arts. For the future of democratic principles, it was another story. November elections of 1932 showed that democracy in Germany was ill-fated by divisions spawned in the aftermath of defeat in World War I. One disrupting factor was economic instability produced initially by wartime destruction, reparation demands, and soaring inflation, and then by worldwide depression and massive unemployment. Another was located in psychological tensions linked to a failure to accept German defeat as due to the superior military power of the Allies, a feeling that the loss had besmirched German honor, and in some circles the conviction that German power had been betrayed from within. There was also mistrust for republican government, especially among military leaders, old aristocratic families, and business interests small and large alike, many of whom regarded the Weimar Republic as foisted on Germans from outside and as unlikely to achieve desired stability.

Within this uneasy setting, the National Socialists (Nazis) garnered about 33% of the vote on November 6, 1932, a decline from an earlier showing but still more than any other party could muster.[6] Shaky though it was, a coalition of right-wing nationalistic groups was formed, and Hitler emerged on top. Hoping to gain majority support for the Nazis, he quickly called for new elections and then engineered authorization for police powers to check "dangers to public security." These powers were brought against the political opposition. Although new elections still failed to give Hitler a clear majority, his policies gained widespread approval and his power was on the rise. By July 14, 1933, it was sufficient for the Nazis to stand as the only legal political party in Germany.

Dissent against Nazi nationalism found expression only in a relatively ineffective minority during the thirties. Specifically, although a "Confessing Church" spoke out in its Barmen Declaration (May 1934) and through individual leaders such as Dietrich Bonhoeffer, Karl Barth, Hanns Lilje, Martin Niemöller, and Heinrich Grüber, a majority of Protestant pastors and laypersons went along with domination of the church by the Nazi state. As for the Catholic side, again individuals such as Bernard Lichtenberg and Alfred Delp would take a stand, but Hitler's successful negotiation of a Concordat with the Vatican (July 1933) stood as an important legitimation of his rule and kept Catholic resistance under wraps. At the same time, neither a Concordat nor Pope Pius XI's protesting encyclical, *Mit brennender Sorge* (1937), prevented Nazi interference in Catholic affairs. And to this summing up, one further point must be added: even where opposition from Christian sources did appear, concern for the plight of Jews was hardly the central motive. Plight there was, too, . . . and had been.

A major plank in the Nazi platform was racial purity. Based on principles of Social Darwinism, natural selection, and survival of the fittest, the aim was to make room for the so-called Nordic-Aryan race, especially as embodied in German people, so that it could achieve its rightful dominion on earth. Crucial corollaries linked with that program. For a start, there are other racial strains, varying in their degree of inferiority but inferior to the Aryan nonetheless. Their very existence, however, sets up a competitive situation that is an obstacle to Aryan supremacy and requires a struggle *(Mein Kampf)* to subdue them. The Jews were singled out as the most virulent threat, so much so that Hitler would portray them as instigating World War II.[7] Some propaganda described Jews as parasites, vermin, beasts of prey—in a word, as subhuman. Other versions offered pictures of a race whose inferiority was deceptively masked behind a subversive cunning which was all too successful at destroying German political and economic life, and indeed bore responsibility for German defeat a generation earlier. Although individual Germans could never see that such descriptions fit all Jews (Aren't there always exceptions?), the net effect still fueled an anti-Semitism that had "the final solution" as its end.

That such attitudes could exist and reap their harvest should no longer elicit innocent astonishment from us Americans, for we are conscious of the racism, white supremacy, and even anti-Semitism that continue to infest our own experience. But still we need to ask: why were the Jews singled out by the Nazis? Ultimately the answers trail on to infinity, but some explanation is to be found simply in saying that the Jews were different and available. That is, however much assimilated into German society, the Jews remained an identifiable and largely compliant minority, and thus they could become a scapegoat to provide the simple explanations craved by the mind where complexity reigns. This suggestion, however, is itself too simple, for the German bureaucracy never obtained total satisfaction in *defining* who or what a Jew might be, a condition necessary for carrying out Nazi plans.[8] Still, even if the Jews were neither identifiable nor available altogether, the process of tracking them down, first in Germany and then all over Europe, never relented until force from the outside prevented it. What could sustain such fervor?

It is well known that bureaucracies are self-sustaining, and it cannot be overemphasized that the Holocaust was a bureaucratic product. Propagandize racial hatred successfully, identify and mark thousands and millions of people, uproot and deport them, confiscate their property for the state, and ultimately annihilate them and make their corpses disappear—such jobs are not accomplished by random acts of violence and hooliganism. You have to organize. Decentralized though it may be, a network of offices and personnel that involves every segment of society is indispensable. The Nazis produced it.

Moreover, the process has to be gradual. It takes time to do all of these things, especially when there is a war to be fought on several fronts simultaneously. Some steps cannot be taken until others have preceded them. Mass murder, replete with gas chambers and crematoria, comes far down the line, but all the more decisively when its time has come. Hitler and his closest associates did envision the physical extermination of Jews from early on. Even so, there was no detailed master plan that timed and controlled every move in advance. The onslaught against the Jews had a structure and a logic of its own, but awareness of that structure and logic grew only as events unfolded blow by blow. Especially for the rank and file who carried out the measures, developments that led toward Auschwitz evolved one at a time, more or less "naturally" out of day-to-day and month-to-month routine as people went about "doing my job."

But why do the job? Fear of reprisal. A long German tradition of obedience to authority. Inability to see a feasible alternative. A sense that successful war efforts really did depend on eliminating a presumed conspiracy of Jews and Communists. All of those reasons played their part. Still, there is another without which they form no sufficient account at all: a tradition of hatred for Jews was strong enough in Germany to make it possible for most Germans to think that they were performing a service for the world by removing an undesirable and unwanted problem-population. And no matter how "understandable" we find the arguments from expedience or ignorance that rationalized a policy of non-intervention against Nazi treatment of the Jews, no matter how much we rightly warn ourselves that it is far easier to judge in retrospect than to act wisely and courageously in the present, still the record stands. Not only were Jewish refugees unwanted almost everywhere, but also Hitler could take comfort from the fact that direct actions against his policies toward Jews, at whatever stage, were exceptions to prove the rule that most non-Jewish populations around the globe remained passive and indifferent, if not implicitly supportive of Nazi aims to destroy European Jewry.

Some people find problem-populations in America, too: the insane, retarded, elderly, ethnic and religious minorities, resident aliens, welfare recipients, criminals, the physically disabled, "radicals," the unemployed, homosexuals, even the not-yet-conceived or about-to-be-born. The specter of "foreigners," if not the Russians then the Chinese or Third World have-nots, haunts others. In a world of scarce resources and teeming desires we ought not to think naively that "final solutions" are beyond us. To restrict such tendencies here requires vigilance about the ingredients in our own backgrounds that might impel us that way. We are not untouched by factors that propelled German minds and Jewish bodies toward crematoria, and it is sound to explore those dimensions further. The first is religious.

Christianity is carved out of Judaism. Moreover, since religions deal with the ultimacies of life, and thus are highly charged with emotion, it should come as no surprise that there is tension between them. Add in the relationship of one faith being born out of the other, but in such a way that they can neither fully embrace nor reject each other, geographically as well as spiritually: volatility escalates.

The Jewish establishment hardly welcomed early Christians with open arms. Animosities rooted in that experience lingered on to color relationships long after Christianity had moved from its status as a struggling Jewish sect, long after it achieved cultural dominance in the West. Likewise, even though the Christian New Testament stresses love for the neighbor irrespective of race or creed, it also contained ingredients to bolster a "teaching of contempt." That teaching carica-tured the Judaism of Jesus's day as being degenerate. It held, too, that the Jews were responsible collectively for killing Jesus and thus for rejecting God through deicide. And it also advanced belief that the dispersion of the Jews from Israel late in the first century A.D.—and perhaps all their subsequent difficulties—was God's punishment for the crucifixion.[9]

Such attitudes do not exist with impunity, as a long history of religiously inspired persecutions, inquisitions, crusades, and pogroms makes clear. The Jew had to *do* nothing to give offense. It was suffi-cient simply to *be,* although the Gentile imagination rarely failed to conjure more specific pretexts for discrimination and violence. And as if fated to be together, the Jewish diaspora and the spread of Christianity tracked each other, even as the Holy Land itself remained a home to both and therefore in a sense to neither. When Matthew had Jesus say " 'I have not come to bring peace, but a sword,' " (Matt. 10:34) he wrote more than he knew. Uneasy tensions between Jews and Christians gnawed away for fifteen centuries, periods of peaceful co-existence mixing with pressures for Christian conversion and poli-cies of isolation and expulsion.

The Protestant Reformation of the sixteenth century brought many changes, but Christian attitudes toward Jews remained largely unconverted. For example, if Martin Luther rightly stands as a hero on many counts, his position on "the Jewish question" is not among them. His pronouncement that, next to the devil himself, a Christian has "no enemy more cruel, more venomous and violent than a true Jew" hardly represents a high point of Christian love.[10] In addition, there is in Luther a logic that perpetually tempts the Christian mind: namely, that misfortune's falling on the Jews is corroborating evidence for the exclusive truth of the Christian faith. When a people rejects God's Messiah, who is also one of their own, no good can come of it. At the very least judgment and punishment will follow.

Four hundred years later, we assume enlightenment has occurred. Perhaps it has. Christian triumphalism is rightly found wanting. Prayer books, religious pronouncements, commentaries on scripture, sermons have been revised to improve Christian images of Jewishness. Interfaith dialogues are held, and at least it can be said that Christian persuasion rarely authorizes persecutions and pogroms any longer. And yet . . . tradition, awareness of history, mistrust, fear that one faith stands as disconfirming evidence for the other, guilt—all of these conspire to keep Jews and Christians at a distance.

My point is not to heap coals on fellow Christians, nor to suggest that Jews embody total innocence, if not perfection. Wallowing in guilt turns too easily into self-consumption or into renewed resentment toward those who stand superior because they have been wronged. There is little profit in either outcome. Likewise nothing is gained by over-idealizing a portion of humanity, when it is clear that no one is immune from being an agent or a recipient of evil. Everything depends on the degree of power that comes to a person or group and on how that power is used, when and where. The proof, for good or ill, is in the acting—nowhere else. Thus, concern about the past means little unless it focuses the future.

Some people predict or wish for the demise of both Christianity and Judaism. My expectation and hope are quite to the contrary, and thus it is crucial to underscore that religion—and specifically a mixture of Jewish-Christian relationships—was a necessary condition for the Holocaust. To hold that view does not deny that those relationships could have developed in ways less destructive. It does suggest that religion, *like every other human enterprise,* is never undefiled or undefiling. That conclusion complicates life immensely, especially if one is convinced—as I am—that many forms of religious life provide insight, release for emotion, and motivation for service that are not only desirable but for which there are no substitutes. Religion is potent. Openness to its innervating power must be matched by alertness to its destructive potential. Otherwise a heavy price is paid.

The Nazis used religious history to obtain precedents for many of the measures, including killing, that they exacted against the Jews. It was something else to find a credible mandate for Jewish annihilation in those sources. No matter. Others were available. They could even intertwine successfully with religious precedents that did underwrite trouble for the Jews. Take anti-Jewish racism, for example.

Christian anti-Semitism and anti-Jewish racism are closely linked, but they are not identical. Anti-Jewish racism began to peak in Germany in the nineteenth century. And what supported it? Philosophical and political theories which held that cultural developments and social behavior—good or bad—are products of physical attributes (i.e., of "blood"). A late-coming but widespread yearning for national unity—"peoplehood"—fostered by political forces which argued that it was socially undesirable, if not biologically impossible, for Jews to be truly German. Suspicion that economic change—ranging from periodic depressions to industrial advances that would threaten old ways of doing business and to urbanization that would undermine old values—were the result of Jewish liberalism and Jewish capital.

The list could be extended, but clearly factors beyond the religious combined in theory and practice to make way for Hitler's policies. Indeed they would have been sufficient in-and-of themselves to unleash mass death in ways that Christian anti-Semitism could never achieve alone. And yet, their power in Germany was inseparable from the religious factor. When the two strands joined up, the required attitudes were ready and waiting. All that was needed was a little more sophistication in propaganda techniques, a little more chaos in the political-economic scene, the right kind of leadership to mobilize the powers of will and bureaucracy. By 1933 the pieces were in place. Apparently disparate forces had become a field that would destroy European Jewry.

Acceptable Years of the Lord?

Persecution of religious minorities. Pre-Civil War enslavement of blacks and post-Civil War segregation. Reservations, if not genocide, for Indians. World War II internment of Japanese-Americans. Atomic bombings. My Lai incidents. It is arguable whether an accumulation of American fury rivals the tragedy of a dozen Nazi years. But link those vestiges from our past with realities that still influence character and opinion in the United States: nationalism, racism, fear, selfish suspicion about economic change, religion that can pit people against each other in spite of its best motives, unrelenting bureaucratization, advancements in propaganda strategies, killing skills, torture. Combine all of these with the proper mix of international pressure and turmoil, particular orientations in leadership, and our on-going proclivity for quick solutions, efficiency, organization, and violence. Odds in favor of our involvement in misery of Holocaust proportions are strong enough that we should recoil with a shudder.[11]

On the other hand, greater concern should go toward a possibility less dramatic but even more likely than our own release of some catastrophe: namely, a tendency toward complacency, indifference, refusal to do all that we can to defend the victimized and oppressed around the world as well as at home. It is not that we are isolationists, fatigued though we may be by worldwide responsibilities and scarred though we remain from Vietnam adventures. Nor is it that we are "know-nothings" who refuse to call injustice, torture, and violated human rights what they are. Still, past performances should leave us wary. American responses to mitigate Jewish suffering under Hitler, for example, have been rightly assessed as "a chronicle of apathy."[12] And it remains an open question whether current policies needlessly trade human lives for business-as-usual.

Vigilance about American proclivities is one order of the day, if we are to stay free and not be swept along unwittingly. But even with vigilance, no purity is left us, for we are strands in an international web more elaborate and delicate than that of the 1930s and 1940s. As never before, the debates and dilemmas involve nothing more or less than *degrees* of guilt and innocence. No difficulty exceeds living with that realization and caring enough about the difference so we preach good news to the poor, proclaim release to captives and recovery of health to the diseased, and set free those who are oppressed. (See Isaiah 61:1 and Luke 4:18.) Nothing is more important either. Proof lives in the contrast between "the acceptable year of the Lord" and the waste laid by the dream of a thousand-year Reich.

As the Nazis entrenched their position and initiated a military build-up, their Jewish policy started its work. Restriction of civil liberties and professional opportunities. Boycotts of Jewish business. Impoverishment through confiscation of property. Outright expulsion of non-German Jews. An arousal of public sentiment against Jews aimed at producing a climate so unpleasant as to make emigration the only option. Riots and violence against Jews broke out from time to time, as in the *Kristallnacht* of November 9–10, 1938, when synagogues were burned, Jewish shops were looted, and thousands of Jews were arrested throughout Germany and Austria. But the worst devastations of these pre-war years were accomplished by slower, less spectacular, and in the long run more efficient means: legislative enactment and bureaucratic enforcement of the Nazi will.

The "Nuremberg Laws," passed unanimously by the Reichstag on September 15, 1935, are a case in point. They contained two basic provisions. First, the "Reich Citizenship Law" stated that German citizenship could belong only to those of "German or related blood." Henceforth, Jews would be subjects only. Moreover, even blood was not a sufficient condition for citizenship. The state conferred it by granting a certificate. Receipt and retention of citizenship, then, depended less on an unalienable right and more on approved conduct. Second, a "Law for the Protection of German Blood and Honor" prohibited marriage and sexual intercourse between Jews and persons of "German or related blood." Also outlawed were employment in Jewish households of German female servants under 45 years of age and display of the Reich flag by Jews.

Such decrees put Jews at the mercy of the German state, but of course the measures could not be fully enforced without a clear definition of what constituted being Jewish. The basic solution was to designate as Jewish anyone having at least three full Jewish grandparents. Also included were persons with two full Jewish grandparents and with any of the following features: belonging to the Jewish religious community as of September 15, 1935, or joining thereafter; being married to a Jew at that date or later; being born from a marriage contracted after September 15, 1935 in which at least one partner was a full or three-quarter Jew; or being born after July 31, 1936, as the illegitimate offspring of extramarital relations involving a full or three-quarter Jew. What to do with persons who possessed lesser amounts of Jewish blood remained a problem and required still further categories and definitions. Suffice it to say that these *Mischlinge* were discriminated against as non-Aryan, but for the most part they escaped death in the gas chambers.

Two footnotes are important. Designation as Jewish was for most people a matter of fate not choice; it had relatively little to do with anything one did. (A person could choose to identify as Jewish, but if one fit the definition of being Jewish that fact was irreversible.) Furthermore, although blood was the issue, a religious test was often decisive in determining the nature of one's blood. To know whether one's grandparents were or were not Jewish might well entail documentation of their religious identifications, or of those of their ancestors. By providing records of births and baptisms, the Christian churches in Germany facilitated the definitional procedures of the Nazis and thereby were implicated early in the destruction process. Unaware of the final solution though they may have been in 1935, the churches nonetheless contributed to that end.

Summer 1939: Hitler's power approached its zenith. His effort to make all Nazi-controlled territory *Judenrein* (clean of Jews) was well under way. Although ever alert to world opinion, Hitler detected *no response* to persuade him that his anti-Jewish policies should not proceed. The situation was similar with his plans to obtain *Lebensraum* (living space) for Germans. Annexation of Austria in March, 1938, was followed by the Munich Conference (September 29–30), which gave Hitler portions of Czechoslovakia in exchange for Neville Chamberlain's "peace in our time." Six months later Hitler occupied the rest of that country. On August 23, 1939, a pact of nonaggression temporarily neutralized the Soviets. Staging was set for invasion of Poland (September 1, 1939) and World War II.

Historians debate the turning points of war. Nevertheless it is safe to say that, with the notable exception of failure to subdue England by air power, the Nazi war machine had things its own way until reversals at El Alamein and Stalingrad in November 1942. The wasting of European Jews also forged ahead—although not quite apace.

Indeed for a year after the war began, the Nazi plan was to continue a policy of forced emigration. Serious consideration focused on turning the island of Madagascar into a Jewish reservation. Only when that option proved impossible, and no similar alternative appeared feasible, did attention move away from expulsion as a solution to the Jewish question. One step carried to its conclusion, the next was always more drastic. If there were no satisfactory ways to export Jews from territory under German control, the Jews would have to be eliminated.

Auschwitz came into being as a concentration camp by Himmler's order on April 27, 1940. In the summer of 1941, its capacity was enlarged and modified. Within the next year it was a full-fledged *Vernichtungslager* (extermination camp) built to last and equipped to employ Zyklon B in gassing people. Death camp efficiency improved in 1943 when crematoria became available for corpse disposal. But it was only in May–June 1944, during the extermination of Elie Wiesel's compatriots, that optimum production was obtained: 12,000 to 15,000 victims per day.

Selective mass killing takes time. But the conclusion to draw is *not* that the Nazis "took their time." However plans for dealing with the Jews evolved, the officials in charge worked persistently, methodically, to implement them. And once the death camps were a reality, Adolf Eichmann and those like him carried out extermination tasks as speedily as technology and circumstance permitted. It is difficult to judge whether the Nazis were more interested in securing their gains of territory and resources against Allied opposition, or whether their top priority was elimination of Jews. Certainly the latter was no afterthought, and the Nazi war aims were never separable from their campaigns against the Jews. Jewish slave labor did provide energy for war industries. But transportation, matériel, and manpower were also diverted from military efforts against the Allies and used instead against the Jews.

Timing and linking of events conspired ironically. Even as the Nazis' eastern front crumbled—indeed as they were pushed back everywhere—their efforts to destroy the Jews were most successful. When Himmler dismantled the Auschwitz crematoria in November 1944, his reasoning was not based altogether on the Russian tanks nearby. It also rested on his conviction that for all practical purposes the final solution had answered the Jewish question.

Expulsion . . . extermination. If the movement from one policy to the other was gradual, what of the intervening steps? An important example occurred on January 20, 1942, at a conference of key Third Reich officials held in the Berlin suburb of Wannsee. Chaired by Reinhard Heydrich, who had been ordered to bring about a "complete solution of the Jewish question in the German sphere of influence in Europe," the conclusion of this gathering was that the European Jews should be evacuated to centers in the occupied east, chiefly Poland.[13] There the able-bodied would form labor gangs. Any survivors—and by understood implication any persons deemed unfit—would be "treated accordingly," the current word for "killed." A massive deportation was soon under way, as trains and transports began to roll all over Europe. Converging on Poland, they fulfilled Hitler's long-standing belief that the only good Jew is a dead Jew.

Two other preludes to the death camps, both of them prior to the Wannsee conference, are also significant. As the Nazis gained control of Poland and other territories with large Jewish populations, one strategy was to rid entire areas of Jews by isolating them in ghettos. (Largest of the ghettos was in Warsaw, which at one time contained some half a million Jews. Uprooted, tormented, overcrowded, starved, diseased, killed in one way or another, their suffering is a story rarely paralleled.) Although ghetto inhabitants were forced to work for the Nazis, the ghetto itself was never to be more than a temporary arrangement. Initially it was to be a way station for the expulsion effort. Later, and especially with the spring of 1942, the ghetto became a staging area for deportation to the recently established killing centers at Chelmno, Treblinka, Sobibor, Maidanek, Belzec, as well as Auschwitz.[14]

Some of the ghettoized Jews, including numerous members of the *Judenräte* (Jewish leadership councils formed at Nazi behest and ordered to facilitate Nazi policy toward the Jews), cooperated openly with the Nazis, hoping that nonprovocation would mitigate Nazi terror or at least increase chances for personal and family survival. The first outcome never resulted; the second rarely. Other Jews dedicated themselves unselfishly to efforts at keeping education, culture, and Jewish tradition alive in the miserable surroundings. Still others resisted violently, the most notable instance being the Warsaw ghetto uprising in April 1943.

Debates ensue over the extent, effectiveness, and significance of Jewish resistance in Warsaw and elsewhere, including the death camps themselves. Some accounts stress Jewish passivity and trustful optimism, religiously motivated. They portray Jews as continual, if unwitting, collaborators in their own demise. Counter-interpretations argue that resistance was varied and widespread. It included not only acts of outright violence, startling that they could occur at all under some of the circumstances where they did appear, but also resistance found expression in the day-to-day determination of Jews to endure without despair.[15] The debates themselves suggest that the truth is mixed somewhere in the middle, but this much is clear: wherever it occurred, violent Jewish resistance lacked the strength of numbers, resources, and especially outside support to be more than a minor roadblock to Nazi objectives. By mid-May 1943, the Warsaw ghetto was liquidated. If that result had not been obtained already, it was soon repeated throughout the ghettos of Eastern Europe.

Although ghettoization was to kill half a million Jews in Poland alone, quite apart from those deported to the killing centers, the Nazi decision to ghettoize was not yet a decision to implement a full policy of extermination. Only with the *Einsatzgruppen* did that phase begin. In the spring of 1941, as plans were laid for invasion of the Soviet Union, Hitler determined that special mobile killing units should be formed. Their task was to follow close on the heels of advancing Nazi troops, round up Jews, and kill them. Four of these more-or-less autonomous teams accompanied the eastern thrust on June 22, 1941.

Each team contained 500 to 1,000 men. Their operations followed a routine. Having gathered a group of Jews together, the Nazis forced the victims to dig a large mass grave. Then, after lining up the Jews along the edge, soldiers mowed them down with machine guns. At least 33,000 Jews were shot in two days at Babi Yar, near Kiev, in September 1941. Along the Russian front, about a million Jews lost their lives in this way during that year alone.

As the invasion and the work of the *Einsatzgruppen* proceeded, a die was cast: Hitler ordered "the final solution of the Jewish question" throughout the European continent. In late July, Heydrich received his orders to carry out measures to assure that the Jewish problem would never have to be solved again. The Wannsee Conference met. Plans unfolded. Camps prepared. Roundups and transports were organized. As the *Einsatzgruppen* moved killers toward their victims, a second prong of attack—bringing victims to their killers—became operational.

When Elie Wiesel says that he does not write about the Holocaust, he means that it is impossible for words to describe or for imagination to comprehend what went on in the death camps. Not that words and imagination can do nothing, but that the magnitude and degree of brutality, suffering, and sorrow are beyond them— that is the point. Keeping such counsel in mind as we complete this outline of Holocaust events, the first thing to note about the death camps is that their horror extended far down the railroad tracks that carried Jews to death. Jammed onto train cars, Jewish deportees faced long journeys in conditions so unbearable that many persons were dead on arrival. Those still living were routed from the cars at the destination. Thereafter practice varied from place to place. In some camps (e.g., Chelmno and Belzec), entire transports were sent directly to the gas chambers. At Auschwitz, which was both a labor and a killing installation, a more elaborate procedure was used.[16]

Men and women were separated; children under fourteen remained with their mothers. Next came selection by a medical official: to the right those fit for work; to the left those who were sick, aged, crippled, and the women with children. The latter group, prodded by Nazi guards and inmate work crews, moved off to the gas chambers and crematoria of Birkenau, the killing-center section of Auschwitz. They were never seen again.

The others, momentary survivors, were left to work, ever subject to further "selections" consigning them to gas and flame. What eventually developed was a slave society heretofore unseen in human history (but perhaps to become more common as the politics of the future seeks "rational" means for handling surplus populations): work was performed quite literally by persons on their way to death, not merely due to sickness or weakness, but because more people were available than were needed. To be sure, the Nazis' efforts were at times counterproductive in that they killed off specialists who could have been used to good advantage. But particularly in the killing centers themselves, the pattern of enslavement-heading-for-death was not uncommon. Substitutes for carrying out most jobs were readily available, so much so that the "reasonable" thing to do was simply to send a worn-out surplus to their death, if not by gas then by planned starvation aimed at getting the most labor for the least cost.

Required work was mainly hard physical labor: mining, road and airfield construction, building the factories of I. G. Farben, or most dismal of all, assignment in the *Sonderkommando* (units whose task it was to remove corpses from the gas chambers, burn them, and clean up the remains). As in all forms of enslavement, inmate status could vary with function to be performed, and treatment could differ accordingly. At least for Jews, however, any respite from death was intended to be only temporary.[17]

Housing and sanitation were abominable. Beatings, hangings, and shootings occurred at the slightest provocation or with none at all. Bizarre medical experiments performed on human guinea pigs, sexual abuse, disease, torture, and constant fear—every affliction of body and spirit was present in abundance. Apart from infrequent acts of kindness from outsiders and the sharing that inmates could—and often did —provide each other, death was the only release.[18]

Death stalked the barracks relentlessly. Every prisoner was vulnerable, but especially the Jews and none more so than those forced to work in closest contact with the gas chambers and crematoria. Nazi intent was that there should be no Jewish witnesses. Their own camp personnel were also sworn to silence, and a vocabulary of euphemisms was used to mask murder. As the German armies retreated, efforts to transfer prisoners to camps farther west was matched by time and energy to destroy the physical evidence of camps left behind.

Most people who entered the killing centers never returned. But there were survivors—thousands of them—a fact both astonishing and not surprising at all. The manufacture of death by the Nazis was efficient. Yet their task was monumental, extremely complicated, and carried out in circumstances that entailed chaos of their own. Where any individual was concerned, however, the chances of survival were precisely that: matters of *chance*. To be sure, individuals were sustained by family members who lived on, by friends—both old and newly made in the camps—by relationships based on nationality, and even by the occasional kindness of a Polish townsperson or a German official. Degrees of individual ingenuity and determination to survive, perhaps so the dead would not be forgotten or so the living would not be forsaken—these factors made a difference, too. Indeed one Jewish survivor-psychiatrist holds that "it was those people who were capable of showing interest in others who, mentally, had the best chance of retaining their individuality—and perhaps also of surviving as integrated persons."[19] Nevertheless, no matter how hard one tried to help others or to save one's own skin, no matter how much hope or faith or will power an individual possessed, most of the crucial factors in survival were beyond personal control: when a person was deported; whether he or she could ward off sickness; whether one might draw a work assignment that would reduce energy output or enable one to obtain better food; whether one could avoid the punishing whims of guards or the caprice of selection.

By late 1944, most of the killing centers were closed. European Jewry was virtually destroyed. Auschwitz remained functional, but it, too, was evacuated on January 17, 1945. With Hitler's suicide on April 30, and the subsequent surrender of Germany on May 7, a chapter ended. But the ending was no ending at all. Far from it. If Europe was not the grave for every Jew who had lived there, many survivors found that it could be called home no more. A new exodus occurred, Palestine the destination. Only after more hardship and bloodshed would Israeli independence be achieved in 1948. Meanwhile other people tried to recover, too—among them Germans who found their country wrecked by Hitler's determination that Germany would win the war or perish. As they rebuilt in the ruins, Germans joined British, French, Italians, Americans in facing or denying, remembering or forgetting as quickly as possible, the rise and fall of the Third Reich.

The Holocaust legacy has no end. It stretches from the prosecution of war criminals at Nuremberg in 1946–47 to the trial of Eichmann in Jerusalem in 1961 to a continuing series of Middle Eastern crises whose roots are in the earth at Auschwitz. It involves searches for ex-Nazis that will move forward to the close of this century, and it includes Elie Wiesel's "Open Letter to President Giscard d'Estaing of France," which protested the release of Abu Daoud, a key suspect in the murder of Israeli athletes at the Munich Olympic Games in

1972.[20] Beyond these global consequences, countless individual stories unfold as well. All of them, in one way or another, are survivor tales. They touch each of us because they are our stories, part of shared history if not direct experience.

Thy Will . . .

So much more to know and tell. And yet historical understanding counts for little in-and-of itself. Everything depends on how it functions, how it is put to use. German scholarship, the finest in the world, did not oppose Nazism decisively. Indeed one of the crucial points of the Holocaust experience is that it transpired in a land of learning and high culture. People who carried out or went along with extermination plans were not ignorant, unsophisticated, and irreligious—not for the most part. To see Hitler and his top associates as barbarians is to miss the subtlety of evil. It is to obscure the fact that good information and good minds can serve the most destructive purposes, partly because such purposes are rarely revealed as such until events have gone too far.

Not that everything would have been well if only people had known more earlier. Knowing more is not identical with knowing better. Paul's self-estimate—"For I do not do the good I want, but the evil I do not want is what I do." (Rom. 7:19)—describes a streak in everyone. Even as we seek and pray for lives transformed beyond ambivalence, even as we are called to rebel against the very pain we inflict, we ought not to be surprised altogether at any terror released by human hands.

Some writers wring their hands as they pronounce that the Holocaust could have been averted if only Christians had been true to their faith, if only the Jews had been less passive, if only popes, presidents, civilized men and women in Germany and around the world had protested more. If only . . . if only. . . . Who could deny it?

At the same time the Holocaust has much to teach about human weakness. Professed allegiance to God or to the highest ideals imaginable . . . apostasy . . . and then a picking-up-of-pieces that permits life to move on. Such is the normal pattern. Amazement is better reserved for the countervailing exceptions of fidelity, resistance, courage, sacrifice—for the fact that there are such exceptions and that they exert power enough to keep alive the dream that human degradation can be checked if not overcome.

The Holocaust brings us close to self-despair. It should. If it does not, we only obscure the desperate character of life by saying our "if onlys" and by failing to acknowledge how morally frail we really are. The risk of seeing ourselves stark naked may be that we never recover. An alternative? " 'I am not telling you not to despair of man,' " says a voice in *The Oath,* " 'I only ask you not to offer death one more victim, one more victory. It does not deserve it, believe me.' " (P. 12)

In 1934, the German director Leni Riefenstahl produced a propaganda film commissioned by Hitler. *Triumph of the Will* remains an important document of the period, but it is the title-theme that deserves attention here. Life's quality depends on the kind of wills that triumph. That struggle, although shaped decisively by our knowledge and ignorance, is decided less by the mind than by the will and the emotions which accompany and motivate its moving. Thinking ranges to infinity and thus to indifference. It is transformed into action beyond itself only as will and feeling intervene. It was not the brilliance of Hitler's thought that enabled him to change all human life to come. By academic standards he was a miserable failure. True, there would have been no Holocaust without ideas, but it took a Hitler's will and then a people's passion to give them flesh and blood. Without the latter, ideas cannot kill.

Likewise ideas and ideals cannot atone and heal, judge and forgive, rebuild and redeem, convey compassion and justice until and unless will and emotion stand—no, *move*—behind them. Knowing what happened in the Holocaust, discerning how an individual such as Elie Wiesel was situated in those circumstances—such insight informs emotion: rage . . . rebellion . . . guilt . . . love. But what, then, shall we *do*—and how? Triumph of the will? A problem with no final solution as long as we live on earth, but surely it does need solving.

A psalm of David tells God that "the enemy has pursued me; he has crushed my life to the ground; he has made me sit in darkness like those long dead." Then it continues: "Teach me to do thy will, for thou art my God! Let thy good spirit lead me on a level path." (Ps. 143:3, 10) Jesus taught his disciples to pray "Thy will be done," and then gave that petition a down-to-earth twist by saying, " 'Not everyone who says to me, "Lord, Lord," shall enter the kingdom of heaven, but he who does the will of my Father who is in heaven.' " (Matt. 6:10; 7:21)

How do things stand with those ideas? Are they empty, like death camp ovens, robbed of will power by a consuming fire that devoured faith and even God himself? Is the Holocaust the death of Judaism and Christianity—the former by God's betrayal, the latter by that of Christians? If so, what options remain? Trust in ourselves, in human-kind, in the benign evolution of nature or the progressive dialectic of history? Anyone willing to look can see that those optimistic hopes did not escape the Holocaust unscathed. Or what if Judaism and Christianity live on? Can they do so unchanged? Should they do so even if they can? Or are they beyond change, trapped—agonizingly so—inside their own confinements of tradition and dogma? And what promise to forestall future holocausts do they contain in any case?

To face such questions takes will power. The conclusion that follows from doing so may be that their answers depend on will power, too. One finality of the Holocaust seems to be that we stand without an ultimate ground of reason under our feet. Such a truth sets us . . . no, it *forces* us to be free, and thereby leaves *will* fundamental for us and for God, too, if he is real.

A line near the end of *The Oath* says: "The moment had come to choose life." (P. 279) For the moment we are all survivors, but the length and quality of our survival together depend on seeing all moments as willful, and on how we make them so. Elie Wiesel's writing, forged in the Holocaust, is a literature of life-choosing. It is a triumph of the will in all the best senses, not least because it reminds us that evil's defeat begins whenever we heal another person, death's finality is refused whenever we enable another to be saved. But will stories told still be forgotten? Will warnings written in blood go unheeded? Will witnesses go unheard and testimonies make no difference? Will the world continue world? Entry into *Night* requires *thy will* to decide.

III
In the Beginning

And God said, "Let there be light"; and there was light. And God saw that the light was good; and God separated the light from the darkness. God called the light Day, and the darkness he called Night. And there was evening and there was morning, one day. (Gen. 1:3–5)

This is the message we have heard from him and proclaim to you, that God is light and in him is no darkness at all. (1 John 1:5)

"Man raises himself toward God by the questions he asks Him. . . . I pray to the God within me that He will give me the strength to ask Him the right questions." (Elie Wiesel, *Night,* p. 14)

Haven't You Heard About It?

A transport arrives at Birkenau, reception center for Auschwitz. Bewildered Jews from Sighet and other Rumanian towns emerge from train-car prisons into midnight air fouled by burning flesh. Elie Wiesel, his father, mother, and little sister are among them. Separated by the Nazi guards, the boy loses sight of his mother and sister, not fully aware that parting is forever.

Father and son stick together. In the commotion, a guard provokes someone within their hearing: " 'What have you come here for, you sons of bitches? What are you doing here? . . . You'd have done better to have hanged yourselves where you were than to come here. Didn't you know what was in store for you at Auschwitz? Haven't you heard about it? In 1944?' "[1]

To the guard's amazement, the Jews of Sighet did not know what awaited them. So near and yet so far away, the final solution had reached them late. Forewarning would have made a difference? At least some persons could have fled for their lives. But forewarning might have counted for nothing, too. The Holocaust, after all, was—

and still is—received repeatedly as news too bad to be believed. Soon enough, however, Wiesel and his father learned what to expect. They were sent "left" by Dr. Mengele, the SS medical official whose baton directed life and death. Normally left was death's way, and for a time their line marched directly toward a pit of flaming bodies. Steps from the edge, a guard's order turned them toward the barracks. But the fire left its mark: "Never shall I forget those flames which consumed my faith forever." (*Night,* p. 44)

Elie Wiesel survived that first night and the days that followed. For ten years after his release, he wrote nothing, sifting and wrestling with the questions that must be asked . . . in the right way. *Night* came first. Originally a manuscript of some eight hundred pages, the English version available since 1960 is a memoir, lean and spare, describing Wiesel's death camp experiences in 1944–45. It begins with a boy who "believed profoundly." (P. 12) It ends with this reflection: "From the depths of the mirror, a corpse gazed back at me. The look in his eyes, as they stared into mine, has never left me." (P. 127)

Some readers find *Night* telling of an anti-Exodus, an anti-Covenant, a triumph for death. The account *is* a reversal of the release of Egyptian slaves into a land flowing with milk and honey. True, Wiesel's story concludes with liberation, but the fundamental action is a journey always deeper into captivity that strips good away. Life-affirming covenants with God disappear, replaced by their opposite: promises of death kept all too faithfully by Hitler. In its images of time and space, in its portrayal of ruined life, the book is a record of death and dying. All of these readings fit, and yet neither singly nor collectively do they exhaust it. *Night* eludes fixed interpretations because of the questions it raises.

Beginnings make all the difference in the world. No less so what we make of them. Our aim is to inquire how things stand between God and humankind after Auschwitz, and especially to explore what Christian testimony is possible in that setting. At first glance, *Night* appears to provide anything but an auspicious beginning, at least if hope is premised on the conviction that Christianity provides trustworthy clues about relations between God and the world. For *Night* probes a void that kills not only Elie Wiesel's parental father, but his faith in God the Father, too.

There would be simpler ways to proceed. The Holocaust could

have been ignored. We could try even now to forget it, and then faith might be easier. Still, notes of rebellion are real. In gut-level honesty, people with religious faith usually want a stance that, if not simply corroborated by experience, is at least able to face its tests without fleeing from them. Faith is strong just to the extent that it can stand aware of, in spite of, even because of facts that count against it. A tall order. It brings a host of complications. For example, the very honesty that propels a person to keep open eyes trained on the dark undersides of existence may also lead one to conclude that religious paths followed once can be taken no more.

Not by his own choosing, Elie Wiesel learned that life can kill trust and hope. Indeed he learned that there are times when it *should* do so, because the alternative is a self-deception that betrays. At this point the line draws finely. Wiesel's objective is never to shatter faith as an end in itself. If his death camp experience forced a form of religious rejection upon him, it also revealed that hopes, dreams, even illusions—religious or otherwise—can be life-giving. To threaten them needlessly is to become a killer. Thus, one of the greatest sins located in the Holocaust is that men and women created conditions in which faith in God's justice, mercy, and love became all but impossible.

What makes the difference, then, between ways in which people —writers especially—put faith to the test? Everything depends on whether the motive is that of tearing down or building up. "One can say anything," writes Wiesel, "as long as it is for man, not against him."[2] That norm and test, however, lead to a second complication.

No individual can work out another's relationship with God. But by what we say and do, we are responsible for shaping options that a person perceives in that area. Religiously speaking, one profound aspect of Holocaust encounters is that they open the options so far, always in the direction of complexity and mystery. That is, the Holocaust forecloses quick spiritual resolutions. Leaving nothing unchanged, it makes faith less "the *assurance of* things hoped for, the *conviction of* things not seen," (Heb. 11:1, my emphasis) and more *a search and quest for them.* It also interrogates other dispositions— atheism and agnosticism, humanism and cynicism—because its range of experience renders everything uncertain except uncertainty itself.

Uncertainty often takes the form of questions. Questions push us back toward beginnings, whether the universe or *Night* is concerned. Can we encounter God in the questions we ask? Can we uplift ourselves through the inquiries we put to God and each other? If we can do so with the Holocaust at the heart of the matter, then Paul may be right: "For I am sure that neither death, nor life, nor angels, nor principalities, nor things present, nor things to come, nor powers, nor height, nor depth, nor anything else in all creation, will be able to separate us from the love of God in Christ Jesus our Lord." (Rom. 8:38-39) And if we cannot, then one search will lead to another. In either case, we shall find that we are in the beginning.

Genesis says that "in the beginning God created the heavens and the earth." At first "the earth was without form and void, and darkness was upon the face of the deep." (Gen. 1:1–2) Then God separated light from the darkness. Day and Night were born; order emerged out of chaos. Other beginnings, recorded in *Night* millennia later, quiz the Creator about darkness and the void. Why were those qualities not erased by God's formative power? Why were they only refashioned, and even then so as to build the possibility of Auschwitz into the world's foundations? Genesis makes a point of calling good that first day's light. About darkness it is silent. At the end of the mythical sixth day, all creation is called good. Even darkness may be included. But the original silence is heavy, at least in retrospect from 1944. Destruction without justification. Waste without reason. Suffering without merit. In a word, *radical evil* stalks what God found good. To speak of the powers of darkness, as we do, should leave us searching: why are they here?

"In the beginning was the Word, and the Word was with God, and the Word was God" (John 1:1)—that is the message that Christians receive. Referring to Jesus the Messiah, it is taken to imply that "God is light and in him is no darkness at all." (1 John 1:5) Jewish questions test those prologues and every Christian touched by them. Elie Wiesel puts to God the question he heard upon entering Auschwitz: "Haven't you heard about it?" And in *Night* his questioning is not meek and beholden. Things are too far out of hand for subservient piety. "I was the accuser," writes Wiesel, "God the accused." (P. 79) And the questions come as steadily as the silence that returns: "Why should I bless His name? . . . What had I to thank Him for?" (P. 43) . . . " 'What are You, my God, compared to this afflicted crowd, proclaiming to You their faith, their anger, their revolt? What does Your greatness mean, Lord of the Universe, in the face of all this weakness, this decomposition, and this decay?' " (P. 77) . . . " 'Where is the divine Mercy?' " (P. 87)

Once Wiesel felt an answer. It formed as he witnessed the execution of three fellow-prisoners. One of them, the center of his concern, was a child:

> Behind me, I heard the same man asking:
> "Where is God now?"
>
> And I heard a voice within me answer him:
> "Where is He? Here He is—He is hanging here on this gallows. . . ."
>
> That night the soup tasted of corpses. (P. 76)

If the scene parallels the crucifixion, remember that no resurrection followed. There was only agonized death, prolonged because the boy's starved body was too light to make the noose work efficiently. The words and scene form a microcosm of the darkness created by the Holocaust. Nevertheless, the image is an enigma. Its meaning is neither single nor announced directly.

Who, what, is dying on that gallows? One child, all children, and Elie Wiesel among them. A world of faith and possibly all worlds of faith, whether they are oriented toward optimism about humanity or toward trust in God. Meanings such as those can be seen, but there is more. For instance, what about the God who is dying in the body of a tortured child?

The child was beautiful, gentle, weak. He may also have been involved in plans for violent resistance, and certainly he showed himself to be tough and courageous in maintaining silence during interrogation torture. Still, he does not quite fit the idea of "The Eternal, Lord of the Universe, the All-Powerful and Terrible" (*Night,* p. 43) that Wiesel had learned as a boy to associate with God. The additional fact that Wiesel never gives up a relation to God—"I did not deny God's existence, but I doubted His absolute justice" (p. 56)—also denies that this death of God is an acceptance of atheism. At most the child could represent a fragment, an aspect of God. And what might that be? The part that transforms the universe. Wiesel writes that the executed boy was "loved by all." (P. 75) The aspect of God that is dying is that which can be loved, at least that which can be loved easily.

A Holocaust Universe can be the outcome of no God at all. It can also be the result of a God who creates, and it can even be linked to a God who watches over and intervenes in history. But it is extremely difficult to relate such a universe to a God providential and moral, to One who organizes and moves history so as to reveal a care "that means life to you." (Deut. 30:20) In witnessing the death of a child, Wiesel suggests that to be with God is to encounter a silent presence—perhaps beyond good and evil, beyond love—who gives life only to leave us alone. That relationship makes the world unsafe: " 'Today anything is allowed. Anything is possible, even these crematories. . . .' " (Night, p. 43)

The answer heard within while Wiesel watched a child die ("Here He is—He is hanging here on this gallows") quizzes more than it resolves. Night brings that process to no resolution. Reasons? Night is truth that must be told to honor the dead, to bear witness for them, to convey the message that darkness can extinguish light. But what are those reasons if not affirmations that life can be good, that we must not forsake it, even if it is so maimed for us that looking in mirrors we see corpses that make us want to drop.

Speaking in God's name, Moses told his people to choose life (Deut. 30:19–20). With Night as back and foreground, all of Wiesel's books explore, refine, and underwrite that command. Always that effort encounters darkness, often so thick that nothing but despondency seems possible. And yet there is always something more. Heavily shadowed, especially in his early works, Wiesel's appeal remains: choose life.

As Wiesel has learned from Moses and his legacy, that conclusion is forever a beginning because it decides nothing specific for anyone. Instead we are moved into troubling questions about ourselves and God. Elie Wiesel thinks that a Jew "defines himself more by what troubles him than by what reassures him. . . . To me, the Jew and his questioning are one." (One Generation After, p. 214) Christianity tries to be more reassuring: the Messiah has come to reveal an unshakable kingdom—so the story goes. But when such claims enter Auschwitz they turn into dilemmas that should lead Christians to opt for a more Jewish identity. As Night moves toward Dawn a step is taken in that direction.

What Do You Want of Me?

Elisha, 18, finds himself in Paris. Liberated from Buchenwald by Americans, his plan is to study philosophy at the Sorbonne "because I wanted to understand the meaning of the events of which I had been the victim."[3] Gad interrupts. This man is a stranger, but Gad knows why he is in Elisha's room. His answer to Elisha's question—" 'What do you want of me?' "—is simple: " 'I want you to give me your future.' " (*Dawn,* p. 27)

Gad needs Elisha's future for the sake of a people. His aim is to make Elisha choose life by engaging in the battle to free Palestine from British rule and thus to achieve the rebirth of a nation, a new Israel. Elisha is moved by Gad's vision. At the same time his religious upbringing, not consumed entirely by the Holocaust, warns him that men and women do not seize holy land with impunity. A Jewish return to Israel, to Zion, still feels like a messianic hope. It is God's prerogative, not his people's. But the experience of Auschwitz is also irrepressible: apparently God will not act, at least not in any way that guarantees Jewish well-being. If there is a God who chooses life, he does so in ways that put it always under threat. Men and women must become their own providence and security. They must become what God never was or what he now refuses to be.

The vision of Gad prevails. It *is* more important to change the world than to interpret it, and the works of the freedom fighter replace those of philosophers. But once called by Gad to play political roles refused by God, Elisha learns how ambiguous it is to choose life: "Well, I said to myself, if in order to change the course of our history we have to become God, we shall become Him. How easy that is we shall see. No, it was not easy." (*Dawn,* p. 42) The ambiguous twist is that choosing life in this particular situation requires choosing death as well.

Elisha, once the possible victim, is now cast as executioner. His order: retribution for the British slaying of an Israeli soldier. His target: Captain John Dawson, a man he does not hate and has, in fact, come to like. Of course, there are circumstances that warrant this Englishman's death. The cause of liberty is just and good; the means necessary to achieve that end are not blameworthy. Israel is worlds away from Treblinka. To equate Elisha's act with that of a *Kapo* or an SS would be blasphemy. But the invalidity of such comparisons is incomplete: "The shot had left me deaf and dumb. That's it, I said to myself. It's done. I've killed. I've killed Elisha." (P. 126)

Killed Elisha? . . . How? . . . In what sense? Elisha's aim is God's eclipse: by taking the prerogative to determine who shall die and who shall live; by deciding that human deeds alone can create and inhabit promised lands, and then only if they show enough strength to shatter resistance and defend against encroachments. So if *Dawn* is the willed continuation of a death of God experienced unwillingly in *Night,* then some of the Jew in Elisha dies as well: that portion which trusts the Lord too much.

Scruples against violence, murder, and execution? Folly in a world where people must be their own providence. To choose life in this Holocaust Universe no one—least of all a Jew—must refuse to kill when survival dictates. Besides, violence, even executions and terrorism, have their own cleansing effect, especially when carried out for a good cause. And they are not only cathartic. They also can be politically effective by showing others that you mean business and that tampering with one's life, liberty, and happiness carries a high price.

And yet . . . it is not, must not be so simple. Elisha's killing brings little release and even less clarity. Oh, he knows that he has executed John Dawson and that he has changed his life and heritage in the process. But to what end and at what cost? History and perhaps God himself had forced Elisha's hand, and there was no better choice than to take history into his own hands. But the result of that action is an ambiguity deepened by the clarity that he had to act in place of God's missing providence. "Ambiguity," says Wiesel, "is the name of our sickness, of everybody's sickness."[4] He could add that it is a sickness that can lead to despair and death as we experience disillusionment at our own hands. He could also add that there is one sickness worse: namely, the sickness of a false clarity that feels no anguish when life is taken away. No, it is not easy to become God . . . unless one becomes a God who lacks sensitivity and decency. That incarnation occurs more than we care to admit.

What do you want of me? Should we be silent? Not ask that question of each other, ourselves, God, or life itself? Or, unable to resist the asking, should we train ourselves to resist expecting answers? The problem is that neither strategy works very well. Life is a series of what-do-you-want-of-me's. Sooner or later most of us thrust them to the sky if not to God. As for answers? Our expectations or the lack of them drag us, however unwillingly, back down to the one suggested by *Dawn:* existence fractures. It will not—cannot be—set right.

Life forces change. Nice if we could read that development as an always upward, progressive movement, but such an evaluation is a luxury all too rare. In most of us the impotence, and thus relative innocence, of youth is replaced by power, and then by tendencies to use it that require massive efforts to keep them from inflicting more suffering than they relieve. Initial anticipations are more optimistic. A Gad or a God or even self-interrogations are first-glanced as more benign. But push does come to shove, and then enough ambiguity recedes to make us aware of the labyrinth we inhabit. We learn with Elisha that life is not easy just because part of the answer to "What do you want of me?" is our own undoing.

What do you want of me? Given that men and women have some capacity to figure out what is going on, that question prods us to seek reasons, explanations, solutions. That prodding, however, is as much burden as it is blessing. Nowhere does Paul speak more truth than when he says that now we see in a mirror dimly and know only in part. But that realization does nothing to calm human restlessness. For we do understand a great deal, and we are convinced that we may understand more, and so we are impelled to keep asking questions and to keep on trying to answer them until we find something that satisfies. The difficulty is that events like the Holocaust defy satisfactions. This ultimate critique of pure reason yields reasons in abundance, but they all raise issues of their own. Consider, for example, some attempts to "explain" the death camps.

At least since the time of Job, human consciousness has been tempted to assume that devastation falls on those who earn it. Likewise with prosperity and peace. At least since the time of Job, human consciousness has also known better, but not well enough to put the former assumptions to rest. Still linked with strands of Judaism and Christianity, themes of retribution and punishment infiltrate efforts to comprehend Auschwitz. Such infiltration kills.

Holocaust-as-judgment? For Jewish failure to obey God's will—a failure understood as collective more than individual—punishment is meted out. By implication the SS becomes God's instrument, not for the annihilation of a people but for their chastisement and correction. The instrument itself, of course, is not without flaw. It also gets justice. Nazi ruins testify that God's judgment is a two-edged sword.

Questions agitate immediately. Does the punishment fit the crime? What kind of God are we dealing with in this scenario? At the heart of the matter, one answer proclaims, is the sovereignty, the holiness, of God. Human life—the existence of the world—is a gift. Nothing forced God to create, and nothing but his own will commits himself ultimately to anything or to anybody. The human story may have started in Eden, and God may have chosen special identity with a particular people. But a permanent rose garden on this earth was not his promise. Divine will and human obedience to it: on those factors everything depends. And what a will it was and is. At times its decisions support our perceptions of rationality, justice, and goodness. At times they confound human standards, and we learn in laughter and tears alike that these words are sound: " 'For my thoughts are not your thoughts, neither are your ways my ways, says the LORD.' " (Isa. 55:8)

The will of God is not capricious might alone. At least the tradition that runs from Moses to the prophets and then on to Jesus and Paul emphasizes the *holiness* of God, and that holiness is not merely naked power. God's holiness-as-power is awesome indeed. Even more so as it includes goodness and righteousness. Those ingredients fill— and frequently dominate—the biblical narratives from start to finish. They are present when great expectations take dust and breathe into it God's image. They are found as God calls Abraham and promises to make him the father of a great people. They project through the exodus of Egyptian slaves, to the covenant between God and his people mediated by Moses and the Law, to the prophecy of Jeremiah and Amos, and for Christians to the conviction that "God so loved the world that he gave his only Son, that whoever believes in him should not perish but have eternal life." (John 3:16)

So the pieces of this Holocaust puzzle are put together as follows: devastation there has been, is, and shall be, but it is not the result of divine wrath alone. There is a corrective purpose, a call to repent and obey. If the correction seems overly harsh, we should remember that life is a gift and that God's holiness is not confined by human desire. God owes us nothing. We are the debtors. What do you want of me? Jews are called to sanctify God's name through adherence to the Law. Christians are taught not only to trust but also to help make real the promise "that in everything God works for good with those who love him, who are called according to his purpose." (Rom. 8:28)

Two additional pieces try to squeeze into this resolution. Although officially disavowed, vestiges remain that make Christians prone to see the Holocaust as God's punishment against Jews for their refusal to accept Jesus as the Messiah. Second, whether related to the first idea or quite independent of it, the emergence of the modern state of Israel is looked on as verification that God brings good out of evil. God's wrath mellowed, and Phoenix-like Israel was reborn out of ashes.

Harsh though they are, these explanations have their comforts. Covenant. Commandment. Disobedience. Punishment. Redemption. One leads to another with simplicity. Those ingredients take an event that seems to explode the moral structure of the universe, and they work it back into a framework that accentuates purpose within early history and even redemption beyond it. For reasons of that kind, a reading of the Holocaust that sees providence as judgment and vice versa always exerts appeal. But the simplicity of such logic is dangerous. To see how, think again about Elisha's dawn.

In theory and practice Elisha's circumstances give him ample justification for killing John Dawson without qualm. More than that, the circumstances seem to make it necessary for Elisha to kill. But the drama in the dawn revolves around some counterpointing questions. Is the execution of John Dawson really unavoidable? Do Elisha's circumstances—or any circumstances—completely justify suffering that may not have to be? Elisha feels the pull of questions like those . . . and then he pulls the trigger. To what end? So that a greater good can emerge? As judgment, as punishment—retributive or corrective—brought to bear against forces that oppose good causes? Or just because an order was given, and orders must be obeyed?

Moments before Elisha kills him, John Dawson is smiling. He tells Elisha that he is smiling " 'because all of a sudden it has occurred to me that I don't know why I am dying.' And after a moment of silence he added: 'Do you?' " (*Dawn,* p. 125) Yes and no . . . and the shot tries to kill twice, taking Dawson and the no at once. The success and failure mix together, and *Dawn,* like *Night,* ends with a mirror-image: "The night lited, leaving behind it a grayish light the color of stagnant water. Soon there was only a tattered fragment of darkness, hanging in midair, the other side of the window. Fear caught my throat. The tattered fragment of darkness had a face. Looking at it, I understood the reason for my fear. The face was my own." (P. 127)

Not remorse or grief. Not even guilt. Fear is what Elisha feels. That quality puts the emphasis on what may yet occur as well as on what has already happened. Is Elisha afraid that one killing will lead to another? Does he fear that killing will be easier and easier until it becomes the most natural thing in the world? So it seems, and with those possibilities Elisha ties us back to tempting "explanations" of the Holocaust. *Like him, we should fear any tendency that makes killing easier and suffering merely understandable.*

Reasons? One appropriate response is that none should be offered. If the reasons are not obvious, no statement or analysis can make them so. On the other hand, we have a great propensity for missing the obvious, and attention to it may help. Rightly, then, we could argue that with every justification of suffering and killing we open ourselves to indifference, and with indifference comes the likelihood that suffering and killing will go unchecked. We could emphasize that such attitudes violate every ethical and religious norm that humanizes life by directing us to love our neighbors as ourselves. Although it would be harder, we might even try to show that we should fear any outlook that justifies suffering and killing because it can undercut self-interest. But all those lines of thought pale in comparison to the best reason of all: the Holocaust itself.

Anything is possible. But hardly anyone alive—let alone the victims—would argue that the Holocaust in-and-of-itself was good. Instead it should not have been permitted. But happen it did, and one crucial ingredient was that people developed, believed, and enforced reasons for killing and justifications for suffering. Any view that allows us to see killing and suffering as natural, expected, as a means to a better end, *without protesting against that same set of perceptions,* plays into the hands of destruction that reached Holocaust proportions once and can do so again. Religious thought is not immune. Unintentional though the result might be, the Holocaust "explanations" that we have examined play into the hands of suffering and killing, just as versions of them contributed to the Holocaust in the first place. They did and do so by taking attention away from the actual plight of human victims, by arguing that the horrible has a justifying logic and that in the long- if not the short-run evil is not as bad as it seems.

To what, then, did Elisha give his future? The answer depends on how he confronts explanations for John Dawson's death. To accept them without recognizing that there are no satisfactory explanations is to invite death to take strides forward. To hear explanations, to follow their logic, and then to refuse to accept them as sufficient— even as one admits that killing deeds have occurred and at times may be unavoidable—that approach is one that could keep us from succumbing altogether.

Relations to God fit a similar pattern. With the Holocaust as measure to help us judge what is for humanity and what against it, we must put to the test what we say or refuse to say about God and to God. *To justify God may be to speak against human life. To protest against God may be to defend what is good. Not simply to accept God's will but to question it long and hard can be essential for sensitizing us to each other.*

One of the best stories about a biblical Elisha tells how that man of God restored life to a dead child (2 Kings 4:8–37). His namesake in *Dawn* appears to stand in stark contrast. And yet no final comparisons can be made so long as the Elishas in us all keep asking "What do you want of me?" and decline to give the future away to explanations that make misery intelligible. The biblical writers remembered a Shunammite woman and Elisha's saving of her son because that man and woman refused to let despondency and grief have the final words. Wiesel's Elisha is memorable not because of his firm convictions in that regard, but because he helps us to see how difficult, and therefore how important, it is to resist temptation to accept too much. That temptation and resistance to it put God and humanity on trial together as we move toward broad daylight and an accident.

Why Should He Want to Kill a Man Who Succeeds in Seeing Him?

On first meeting Gad, Elisha told him that " 'the future is of limited interest to me.' " (*Dawn,* p. 26) Did his experiences with Gad and his post-execution struggles make the future urgent for Elisha? Uncertain. We do know that Elie Wiesel rounds off his beginning trilogy with the French-titled *Le Jour (Day)*. But even that work is not the emergence of light out of darkness, not without ambiguity.

Both *Night* and *Dawn* reveal that the swords of politics and history cut many ways; once one has experienced this kind of destruction *Day* asks: "Is life worth living at all?"

His present and future overwhelmed by what he has witnessed in the past, another in a long line of young people—all the same, all different—doubts that he can endure his Holocaust survival. The world will not be changed; the dead cannot be brought back to life, even though they haunt the living too much, creating feelings of guilt, frustration, anger, and rebellion that make joy and happiness all but impossible. In spite of the fact that he has friends, and even a woman who loves him, the young man's life is "the tragic fate of those who came back, left over, living-dead."[5] And so, not only because he feels that " 'I am my past,' " (*The Accident*, p. 66) but also because he knows that his inability to move beyond makes others suffer, this person senses that life will demand him to lie in ways that he has neither the desire nor the strength to sustain.

Not feeling well, worn out by the heat and a reporting job that seems of no consequence, the young man still manages to keep his date with Kathleen. They decide on a film. Then, crossing a busy street, the young man is struck and dragged by a car: *Le Jour,* rendered in English, becomes *The Accident.* "On the fifth day I at last regained consciousness. . . . I felt alone, abandoned. Deep inside I discovered a regret: I would have preferred to die. An hour later, Dr. Russel came into the room and told me I was going to live. . . . That I was still alive had left me indifferent, or nearly so. But the knowledge that I could still speak filled me with an emotion that I couldn't hide." (Pp. 22–23) Nurtured by friends, continuing under the care of a doctor who takes death as a personal enemy, life returns to be chosen again.

As Wiesel weaves past and present together, it remains uncertain whether the accident was premeditated. It is clear, though, that the young man comes to interpret the accident as a choice of death. Thus, *The Accident* is no melodramatic account of bungled suicide. Instead it probes more deeply as Wiesel catches his character in between: In between recognizing how much he wanted to die and how much others want him to live; in between sensing that he will live on and yet not seeing how to do so well. "The problem," Wiesel proposes, "is not: to be or not to be. But rather: to be and not to be." (P. 81) At least for survivors, life conspires to make people choose it; suicides are exceptions that prove the rule. And therefore the issue for most persons, most of the time, is not whether to be but what to be, and we face the latter always in the midst of tragedy. Such nothingness threatens to consume us. Not so much by leading people to take their own lives, but by making us living-dead who pass those qualities to others.

Why does life come to so much grief? If not through wrongdoing, judgment, and punishment alone, then because suffering itself is instructive and redemptive? It teaches us our limits and possibilities alike, and should it be prolonged unto death, accompanying heroism and even martyrdom can lift the spirits of men and women everywhere. The suffering servant . . . the dying Christ . . . a God pained by his own love of earth . . . images like those come down through the ages to suggest that suffering means more than meets the eye. No doubt such outlooks contain some truth. What man or woman has not learned some constructuve lesson via pain, or communicated a helpful strength to others by enduring or dying well? Yes . . . and then *but.*

The Accident was caused by a "yes, but." It occurred because too much suffering had been witnessed to balance out instructive or redemptive scales. Martyrs, saints, . . . maybe even Saviors . . . " 'are those who die before the end of the story.' " (P. 53) Such is the response when Kathleen asks her friend—long before the accident— whether suffering leads to saintliness. He thinks instead that there is " 'a phase of suffering you reach beyond which you become a brute: beyond it you sell your soul—and worse, the souls of your friends— for a piece of bread, for some warmth, for a moment of oblivion, of sleep.' " (P. 53) To be sure, it is possible to say that a person broken by suffering is simply one who cannot "take it." And no judgments hit harder than the self-doubts that intrude when survival or well-being seem to follow from a "giving in" that a better use of will would not have tolerated.

Paul promises that "you can trust God not to let you be tried beyond your strength, and with any trial he will give you a way out of it and the strength to bear it." (1 Cor. 10:13, The Jerusalem Bible) Who has the burden of proof? Is it only to those whose faith is sufficiently strong that the promise is made good? Either that, or we have to see death itself as the Messiah. Both views have problems. On the one hand, faith is neither necessary nor sufficient for earthly survival. On the other, it is neither necessary nor sufficient for losing one's life in Auschwitz or anywhere else. Beyond that, death-as-

Messiah so often comes too late, and thus can be no Messiah at all. To die after one's life is in pieces may well be a release. But even if there is life beyond the grave, such a way of finding Paul's promise fulfilled is ironic, if not callous and cynical.

The Accident signals that every person has a breaking point. Individually no one knows where it is, not until too late. Maybe things are better that way, because then we are really left responsible. But like God's promises, responsibility is a mixed blessing because it brings so much guilt in its wake. To be sure, all adults have good reasons to feel guilty. But just as we overestimate the value of suffering, so we may assess guilt unfairly and therefore in ways that harm. And not only with respect to each other. God figures in as well, in spite and because of the fact that "man prefers to blame himself for all possible sins and crimes rather than come to the conclusion that God is capable of the most flagrant injustice." (*The Accident,* p. 45)

Do we honor God and ourselves by holding him blameless? Or is it just a fearful hope that leads people to absolve God of sin? The victim of the accident has seen too much to pursue either course any longer. He understands that to hold God blameless only intensifies despair that is already more than many human hearts can bear. His desire to live is not unequivocal, but it is sufficient to rule out any piety that legitimates the ways of God at humanity's expense. And thus the abuse endured by Sarah, namesake of a people's mother, indicts God harshly.

"Whoever listens to Sarah and doesn't change, whoever enters Sarah's world and doesn't invent new gods and new religions," writes Wiesel, "deserves death and destruction." (P. 96) Sarah's world? In *The Accident* it is that of a Paris prostitute, but as the accident victim relives his encounter with her, he and Sarah are taken back to an earlier time and place. That Sarah's world is built on a question: " 'Did you ever sleep with a twelve-year-old woman?' " (P. 97) And the place where it was asked and answered with a vengeance was in the special barracks of Nazi concentration camps, erected for the camp officers' diversion.

A biblical tale says that God once told Moses that " 'man shall not see me and live.' " (Exod. 33:20) God's word to Moses is usually interpreted to mean that a human person cannot see God and live because of the disproportion between the might and righteousness of God on the one hand and the weakness and sin of men and women on the other (see Isaiah 6:5). Indeed the fact that God is hidden, obscure, revealed to us indirectly, is often seen as a form of grace that enables human life to have its chance. *The Accident* is premised on ideas of that kind, but Sarah's world turns them and makes God's warning say something more:

> Why should He want to kill a man who succeeded in seeing Him? Now, everything became clear. God was ashamed. God likes to sleep with twelve-year-old girls. And He doesn't want us to know. Whoever sees it or guesses it must die so as not to divulge the secret. Death is only the guard who protects God, the doorkeeper of the immense brothel that we call the universe. (Pp. 97–98)

That estimate cuts even more deeply when Sarah discloses that her purity as a victim is forever compromised: she recalls that she sometimes felt pleasure in those barracks, and probably survived because of it.

What about this round of question-and-answer? Doesn't it just sour already bitter experience? Wouldn't it be better to reject the implication that God is a cosmic sadist and keep on affirming, in spite of the world, that "God is light and in him is no darkness at all"? Or would it be better to refuse both options? The first because it is morally intolerable; the second because concentration camp brothels disconfirm the claim except for Gods too weak to make their goodness matter. Wouldn't it be better to embrace no personal, purposive God at all? Or would it be better still just to stop pursuing such lines of thought completely?

The Accident does not answer straight out. Its victim is alive in a hospital at the end, or he is even released and telling his story from an unidentified time and place. The truth is that we don't know whether this man's questions raised himself toward God, or if they did what he discovered in the process. We do know that Elie Wiesel survived *The Accident* to write another day, which is to say that he persists in tracing the issues raised in the beginning of his authorship and indeed of the world itself. But why? What is to be achieved by such effort?

> "Stories."
> *"But there must be more to it than that."*
> "Yes, there is more to it than that."

"What, then?"

"I am afraid of what will happen if the effort ends."

"What will happen?"

"Nothing."

"And that makes you afraid?"

"Exactly."

"But what if we make the effort?"

"I am still afraid."

"Why?"

"Because even in making it we may stop and rest with a conclusion."

"But isn't that the point, to draw a conclusion?"

"No, that's not the point."

"Then what is?"

"There isn't any . . . except to keep asking 'What's the next step?' . . . except to keep wondering 'And yet? . . . and yet' . . . except to keep willing 'In spite of . . . because of . . .' "

"So how does God figure into this equation?"

"He doesn't, at least not clearly enough, and that's what makes our lives hang in the balance of our asking."

"Are you suggesting that encounters with God—whether and how we have them—make the future?"

Night . . . Dawn . . . Le Jour/The Accident . . . their questions set an agenda for encounters between Creator and creature after Auschwitz. Specifically for those who claim to encounter God through Jesus of Nazareth. Desolation in the Kingdom of Night. Despair produced by dawn's ambiguity. An evening accident and a tortured spirit who will leave a hospital only half healed in the light of day. These are beginnings that the Holocaust beckons us to share. They show that nothing about the first day in the beginning was quite as good as God pronounced it—or that devastating differences of opinion were destined to follow from the original separation of light and darkness. But the message of those differences is not to shirk responsibility by blaming God. It is rather to explore how crucial is human responsibility in a world which not only lacks enough insurance for the good but even permits our doing—as well as thinking—the unthinkable. That message is enough to make one give up. And yet . . . ?

IV
Against Despair

Moses looked; there was the bush blazing but it was not being burned up. "I must go and look at this strange sight," Moses said, "and see why the bush is not burned." (Exod. 3:2–3, The Jerusalem Bible)

We are in difficulties on all sides, but never cornered; we see no answer to our problems, but never despair. (2 Cor. 4:8, The Jerusalem Bible)

And so, because never in human history have people had more reasons to despair, and to give up on man, and God, and themselves, hope now is stronger than ever before. It's irrational; it's absurd, of course. But it may be a way of achieving a certain victory. Not absolute victory. A small measure of victory. (Elie Wiesel, *A Small Measure of Victory,* p. 5)

Nothing Has Changed?

As the previous chapter neared completion, I visited Elie Wiesel in New York City. Purim was at hand. This Jewish holiday, based on events in the biblical book of Esther, takes its name from the lottery method used by Haman to determine the day on which all Jews in the Persian empire were to be exterminated. Mordecai, a deported Jew in the service of King Ahasuerus, had refused to bow before Haman after the king had commanded that all servants should do so. In return for this affront, Haman planned genocide. But—by chance?—his wishes did not come true.

Esther, Mordecai's cousin and adopted daughter, had found her way from the king's harem to the position of queen. She had obtained this position without anyone's suspecting she was Jewish. No assimilationist, however, this Esther. Upon learning of Haman's order, she invited him and the king to a series of banquets, and at the auspicious moment interceded with the king on behalf of Mordecai and her people.

With some of the best irony that the Bible offers, the story continues:

> In a rage the king rose and left the banquet to go into the palace garden; while Haman, realising that the king was determined on his ruin, stayed behind to beg Queen Esther for his life.
>
> When the king returned from the palace garden into the banqueting hall, he found Haman huddled across the couch where Esther was reclining. "What!" the king exclaimed. "Is he going to rape the queen before my eyes in my own palace?" . . . So Haman was hanged on the gallows which he had erected for Mordecai, and the king's wrath subsided. (Esther 7:7–8, The Jerusalem Bible)

Not only that. King Ahasuerus gave the Jews permission to arm for self-defense, to annihilate any who attacked them, and even to plunder the possessions of their enemies. The Jews seized the opportunity—killing seventy-five thousand opponents on one occasion—except that they took no plunder. Instead the feast of Purim is also a special occasion for giving to the poor.

Purim was a good time to visit with Elie Wiesel, and he took pleasure in telling me that when he accompanied his son, Elisha, to the synagogue festivities that evening, the children would use noise makers to blot out the name of Haman when the story of Esther was read. But as we talked about the biblical account, a darker side emerged. The Hebrew text, Wiesel told me, refrains to speak of God. It is unique in the Bible for that reason, and thus it raises the question "why?" Perhaps, Wiesel suggested, because miracles happen only when God is not too close, only when he is hidden or even absent. Does that idea make any sense? What could it mean?

Such questions are not idle speculations. They require reckoning with one's own beliefs and hopes—or setting them aside out of indifference or lethargy, all of which involve a giving-up-too-soon. Elie Wiesel is a man of sadness, not simply because he witnessed the Holocaust's destruction, but also because he finds people complacent, unstirred by the challenges and dilemmas of their own lives. His own writings, emerging from intensity that is both the burden and the responsibility of Holocaust survivors, aim to put people off their guard. Always lacking answers but never failing for questions, he lays out problems not for their own sake but to inquire, "What is the next step?" Reaching an apparent conclusion, he moves on. "And yet? And yet." . . . "In spite of this, something more must be noted." . . . "How

is one to believe? How is one not to beleive?" . . . Those are the forms
of his thinking. They always reject easy paths in favor of hard ones.

It is frustrating, maddening to read and meet Elie Wiesel. He will
not hold still, and he makes a point of saying that he is not afraid of
contradictions. For some people, Wiesel's writings are evasive. He
won't draw any single conclusion from Holocaust facts and stick with
it neat and clean. The result, some believe, is that he lays out too many
options. He permits people to believe anything they want, or he clouds
things over and mystifies what should be clear and distinct. Such
criticisms reveal the risky path that Wiesel has chosen. It affirms:
more important to seek than to find; more important to question than
to answer; more important to travel than to arrive. His point? Dangerous to believe what you want to believe. Deceptive to find things too
clear just as it is also dishonest not to strive to bring them into focus.
Insensitive to recognize that there is always more to experience than
our theories admit even though we can never begin to seek comprehension without reasoning and argument. And so Elie Wiesel tells his
stories, and he will not—cannot—draw conclusions for his readers.
Nor can he prevent them from doing so in his stead—that is the
chance he takes in hoping that he can keep people moving to give life
and not kill it. Such a course should be familiar to anyone who tries
to follow Jesus. With that recognition in mind, I remember my Jewish
friend telling me that what his books say is less important than what
they lead readers to say about themselves.

"The Jew," says Wiesel, "can help mankind by helping Jews
or mankind but only as a Jew."[1] His way is to tell his Jewish stories in the hope that they will bring a miracle that averts human
self-destruction. But everything depends on how and to what degree Jews learn what "being a Jew" means, especially after Auschwitz. The point holds for Christians, too. The Holocaust should
push us to discover and struggle with the meaning of "being a
Christian" not simply in the twentieth century but in the first
A.D.: Anno Domini and After Dachau. For there is a sense in
which the Holocaust takes Christians back to the beginning in
ways akin to the vision that Elie Wiesel holds for his fellow Jews:
"While man cannot begin—only God can do that—it is given to
man not to accept an imposed end. To begin is not in the realm of
man's possibilities; only to begin again, over and over again."[2]

Asked about the relation of his tales to each other, Wiesel says that

they move like concentric circles in and around *Night.* The strategy
is to take men and women in and out of darkness in ways that explore
"Why should people care?" Despair portrayed in his first three books
lives in a God-forsaken world. With protest against God as a common
motif, they indict God severely. But what about the next step? Should
a Christian have anything to do with such attitudes? Doesn't the
Christian belief that the Messiah has come, that he lives and rules as
a resurrected Lord, make all the difference? Doesn't it render protest
to God unwarranted and unseemly? Or should we Christians find
ourselves included when Elie Wiesel says: "During and after the
Holocaust, it was impossible for any Jew not to choose defiance as a
means of transcending despair"? ("From Holocaust to Rebirth," p. 5)

What should be the next step? One is to see how Wiesel gets from
Night to *The Gates of the Forest* and three other major novels that he
has published thus far. Wiesel's first works travel through the destruction of a supportive universe, into the ambiguity, despondency, and
nothingness that accompany a realization that men and women must
be their own providence. Life almost succeeds in fulfilling a choice to
cancel itself, but failure on that score becomes a turning. That turning,
however, remains blurred. The silence of God, the moral emptiness
of the Void, and the destructive Kingdom of Night—all shadow
reasons for living.

Nonetheless, Wiesel asserts, to be Jewish is "never to give up—
never to yield to despair."[3] That affirmation is a categorical imperative. It applies in relation to human persons and God alike, irrespective of the temptations toward despair that they provoke. Such a
commandment is exceedingly difficult. To keep it Wiesel must wrestle
long and hard, for and against the Jewish tradition that retains norma-
tive qualities for him and thereby for and against God and humankind
together. Thus, effort to discover and to create trustworthy reasons
and resources against despair is one path that joins together the
spiraling concentric circles formed by his major novels.

> When the great Rabbi Israel Baal Shem-Tov saw misfor-
> tune threatening the Jews it was his custom to go into a certain
> part of the forest to meditate. There he would light a fire, say
> a special prayer, and the miracle would be accomplished and
> the misfortune averted. Later, when his disciple, the celebrated
> Magid of Mezritch, had occasion, for the same reason, to

intercede with heaven, he would go to the same place in the forest and say: "Master of the Universe, listen! I do not know how to light the fire, but I am still able to say the prayer." And again the miracle would be accomplished. Still later, Rabbi Moshe-Leib of Sasov, in order to save his people once more, would go into the forest and say: "I do not know how to light the fire, I do not know the prayer, but I know the place and this must be sufficient." It was sufficient and the miracle was accomplished. Then it fell to Rabbi Israel of Rizhyn to overcome misfortune. Sitting in his armchair, his head in his hands, he spoke to God: "I am unable to light the fire and I do not know the prayer; I cannot even find the place in the forest. All I can do is to tell the story, and this must be sufficient." And it was sufficient. God made man because he loves stories.[4]

With his version of a legend, Elie Wiesel introduces Gregor, another Jewish survivor. Gregor has found refuge with a Christian, Maria, who was once a servant for his now annihilated family. The price for safety is silence, and Gregor becomes a mask. Pretending to be a deaf-mute nephew who has come to live with his aunt, Gregor walks safely the streets of a town in which no Jew is safe. But the disguise cannot, does not, last. Cast in the role of Judas for the town's Passion Play, Gregor finds that appearance is reality. Citizen actors turn mad. They begin to beat him to death.

Gregor saves himself by breaking his silence, by telling his own tale. With time bought by the power of words, he manages escape to the forest where he is able to join a group of resistance fighters. Hiding in the woods, raiding out of them, Gregor fights not merely for survival but also to locate the *why*—and thus the *how*—of friendship. Later, living in New York and married to Clara (whom he met in the forest resistance), Gregor finds that their life together focuses on the missing, the absent, the dead—Gavriel, Leib, Yehuda—all of whom taught worthy visions of life only to have them ended violently.

Love cannot grow in those surroundings, at any rate not love for the living. Gregor will leave Clara. Maybe then the past, present, and future can separate themselves as well. But the book ends with Gregor saying a prayer for Leib, his friend and Clara's love, and with Gregor finding renewed determination to breathe life into his relationship with Clara.

How does this change occur? The answer stays masked, but there are hints. *The Gates of the Forest* lets in some light: Gavriel, for example, one of Gregor's companions in the forest. Bearing an angel's name which means "man of God," he is one of the numerous characters in Wiesel's books who are driven to a form of madness by what they have witnessed. This madness Wiesel calls mystical and moral. Far from being insanity it is an obsession with life pitted against every rationale and rationality that results in needless suffering. It is a passion born because and in spite of despair. It yields compassion for others even when—or precisely when—defeat seems inevitable. More than once, Gregor heard Gavriel cry out against injustice: " 'If this is God's will, then deny it! The time has come for you to impose your will upon His, to pin Him to the wall. You'll have to pay, you say? What of it? You'll be damned? So what?' " (P. 57) Gavriel sacrificed his life to divert a Nazi search party from Gregor's hiding place.

Gregor has lived for a long time with the conviction of God's guilt, or with the recognition that the Messiah is not coming, which is the same. But where does one go from there? That is the question. One of its results is a suffering that dwells on the past. That outcome is not altogether wrong; to forget would be a worse fate. But the need is to grasp the message of Yehuda: " 'It's inhuman to wall yourself up in pain and memories as if in a prison. Suffering must open us to others. It must not cause us to reject them.' " (P. 180) That message points us to God and other persons alike, and one way that its tasks can be tackled is by telling "the story." Words are essential. So are deeds, and once more Yehuda sees truly: " 'An act of love may tip the balance.' " (P. 178) Through such acts the Messiah comes—or not at all.

In the witnessing and dreaming aftermath of a Hasidic celebration that he has chosen to attend without fully understanding why, Gregor hears the past speaking with urgency as he faces his own choice of life or death in relation to Clara. Its message—turn suffering into protest and love for others—heard often before and yet never before his decision to leave her, informs Gregor's life. It intensifies a reason, a passion, by which to live. Thus, Gregor replaces his non-Jewish name with that of Gavriel. In defiance of God's will—in refusal to let events take their own course—he seizes the chance for revived understanding between Clara and himself, if not for reconciliation in tension with God.

What about "the story" that Christians tell, especially its Easter chapters about resurrection and new life? Doesn't it have different implications and results? To believe that Jesus spoke truly when he said, " 'I am the resurrection and the life; he who believes in me, though he die, yet shall he live, and whoever lives and believes in me shall never die' " (John 11:25–26)—does not that belief entail conviction that no protest and only praise should be the Christian's expression to God? For even if things are terribly out of whack on earth, the kingdom beyond death will set things right and all will be well. Unfortunately, things are not so simple. History's carnage, brought to a head but not climaxed by the Holocaust, no longer makes it credible to sing only with joy and thanksgiving Easter hymns that spite the sting of death and the grave's victory.

Holocaust smoke casts a pall over the empty tomb. Reasons? As a Rebbe tells Gregor, " 'Auschwitz proves that nothing has changed, that the primeval war goes on. Man is capable of love and hate, murder and sacrifice. He is Abraham and Isaac together. God himself hasn't changed.' " (*The Gates of the Forest,* p. 192) And yet that is not the whole story either. For the Christian proclamation is that something new has occurred, things have changed: the suffering, death, and resurrection of Jesus make plain as never before or since God's loving intentions toward men and women. But pause. The proclamation is the problem. Whatever these loving intentions may be, Auschwitz shows that too little has changed, and the Christian's dilemma—and cause for protest—is precisely in the contradiction: believing that all things are being made new and seeing that really they are not.

Even this interpretation is not the whole story. When Paul tells Christians that "if in this life only we have hoped in Christ, we are of all men most to be pitied," (1 Cor. 15:19) he points us to a kingdom that is not of this world. There seeing and believing shall be one and the same, and "God will wipe away every tear from their eyes." (Rev. 7:17) But whether this new condition involves all men and women or only a chosen few, questions should be asked about it. What does God's wiping away of tears imply? These tears to be wiped away are not tears of joy, but rather expressions of grief, sorrow, even rage and anger—all the result of destructive events that have been allowed to happen. Will the circumstances in which tears are wiped away be so dazzling that people will just forget what went before, or will the wiping away have the erasure of human memory as its condition?

Unless God persuades or transforms our minds and hearts in ways that could have happened earlier but did not, murmurings will be found in heaven once people discover again who they are and what world they have come from. But if that transformation occurs, at what price? By treating the past as though it never happened? By adjusting minds so that present experience makes the past of no account, makes it something canceled out, gone forever? If heaven makes everything sweetness and light, that reality should be enough to bring new tears to our eyes, new protests to our lips. Conclusion: Under no circumstances can God be trusted simply, completely. Reasons? His promises are full of twists that rarely fit what they seem to mean. As Isaac knew better than anyone when his life was spared by the same God who had demanded its sacrifice, the one God is not only one but many-in-one. Total peace and quiet are strangers to him, and thus they elude us as well.

And yet . . . what is the next step? For Christians it is to go on telling the story in the best way they know how. It is to affirm that the grave is not the victor, that there are chances for new life which are worthwhile even if they cannot undo the past, that individuals can be changed for the better even if the world stays too much the same, that joy can be real and right—on earth and in heaven—even if always precarious. The next step also involves trying to obey Jesus's commandments just because they can be a form of madness that rebels against injustice, which includes Christian tradition that has maimed and killed and which indicts God when he permits too much. Taking steps like those, it can be discovered that a spirit of Christian rebelliousness constitutes one vital form of praise rendered to the God who gives us life that can and therefore must be good.

Burned but not consumed. The bush that confronted Moses is a symbol for the Jewish people themselves. If we approach it in that light, what is found when Moses looks to see why the bush still stands? *The Gates of the Forest* hints that one ingredient is a defiant faithfulness rooted two ways. First in a teaching of Gavriel, who "used to say that the difference between Christians and Jews was that for Christians everything that comes from God is good and everything evil bears the mark of man; the Jews, however, press their search further and more blasphemously, crediting God with evil as well as absolution." (P. 101) Second in a vow that says: "Master of the Universe, I know what you want; you want me to stop believing in you . . . But you won't succeed, you hear me, you won't succeed!" ("From Holocaust to Rebirth," p. 5)

Our world risks consumption when followers of the resurrected Jesus do not show Christian feeling that burns with Jewish fire. If we Christians believe that God chose to defy death through Jesus of Nazareth, we should understand too that death itself is of God's making and that it takes an absurd toll without ceasing. An individual's earthly life should never end? No, that is not the point of protest. A life—long, full, and satisfying—should not be given up without regret, but such death can be greeted with equanimity. Less so where death is untimely, violent, pain-filled, empty.

To follow Jesus is to be death-defying before every force that *wastes* human life. How should that faithfulness be carried out? One way is Purim's example: combat the despair of extermination decrees by *giving*. Steps like those trace back to an earlier place. Back to *The Town Beyond the Wall* . . . and to Calvary.

Why Does God Insist That We Come to Him by the Hardest Road?

Calendars and seasons intertwine. Winter turns to spring—and hope springs eternal?—in the time of Purim and Passover and as Lent becomes Good Friday and Easter. The latter is a second Passover for Christians, a new covenant to underscore God's intentions to liberate and redeem. Yet seen through what precedes and follows, the proclamations of Easter become strange indeed. They border on madness.

The difficulty is not located simply in the claim that death has been conquered. Although empirical evidence against that claim is massive, Christian faith always lives in spite of the canons of public verification. Rather the problem lies in comparison between the conviction that God took with utmost seriousness the death of one Jew long ago and the fact that he was apparently indifferent to the death of six million in our own time. An oversimplication? If it is, complexity intensifies the madness. Consider, for instance, the last days of Jesus's life.

There are some moments of triumph. Entry into Jerusalem on

Palm Sunday. Cleansing of the temple. Mainly though, it is a time of shadows. Fear, greed, indecision, stealth, deceit, betrayal—a catalog of frailty and corruption emerges from that week. God is willing to let it all unfold. Jesus goes to the Garden of Gethsemane to pray that a different plan might substitute, but what did he hear in return? Gospel writers are mute. So when Jesus expressed his wishes, or even qualified them with a " 'nevertheless, not as I will, but as thou wilt,' " (Matt. 26:39) did empty silence fill the night? And what about later on when—what word shall be used?—Jesus spoke, cried out, questioned, protested: " 'My God, my God, why hast thou forsaken me?' " (Mark 15:33–37)

Troublesome words. Omitted in Luke's narrative. John's Gospel, too, records them not at all. Instead he writes that Jesus said, " 'It is finished'; and he bowed his head and gave up his spirit." (John 19:30) Matthew includes the question, softened by saying that Jesus "yielded up his spirit." (Matt. 27:45–50) Mark's account, the earliest, does more to let the cry stand out, adding only that Jesus "breathed his last." (Mark 15:37) One theory is that Jesus's question is his recollection of the twenty-second Psalm, which begins as a lament and ends with praise for God and trust in him. That interpretation could be true, but the question stays a question nonetheless. God's silence remains, too, or else we are left to hear God lamenting and protesting and crying out to himself. In either case, there must have been an easier way, a clearer way, a better way for making divine intentions known. And what was the point of it all? To let history keep repeating itself world without end? Was God really serious about making all things new in Christ when Calvary could lead to Chelmno?

If God suffered in Christ—as a blood sacrifice to appease his own wrath over human sin, as an expression to show that nothing can separate the world from his love, or even as a sign of atonement for his own injustice toward men and women—for whatever reason, that suffering pales in magnitude before the outrage of a Holocaust. Unless we see God suffering wherever men and women suffer. But what if that is the case? It doesn't make sense anymore than a view that extols the suffering of God in Christ as though it were more vast, and therefore more significant, than the accumulated pain of the world before and since. For if a suffering God is only a suffering God, then God help us. And if God suffers with us, when the suffering we

experience does not have to be, then what is going on here? Even if
there is a method in the madness, the right question will still be: why
does God insist that we come to him by the hardest road?

"Pedro broke into applause, laughing: 'I like you, my friend!
You're trying to drive God mad. That's why I like you.' I thought:
And God too is trying to drive me mad."[5] Come visit *The Town
Beyond the Wall*. Discover that undermining of indifference is the
method in the madness. Once Michael's home, this place is now in the
vise of Communist victors over Nazi tyrants. Secretly returning to see
whether anyone can be found in a ruin, Michael stands before a house
where a face watched silently while Jews were deported ages ago. The
face, seeking a hatred from Michael to match its unacknowledged
guilt, informs the police. Michael finds himself imprisoned in walls
within his past, tortured to tell a story that cannot be told: there is
no political plot to reveal; his captors would never accept the simple
truth of his desire to see his home town once more; his friend Pedro,
who returned with him, must be protected. Michael tries to hold out.

"This, this was the thing I had wanted to understand ever since
the war. Nothing else. How a human being can remain indifferent."
(P. 159) Madness has many expressions. Indifference is one, and
Michael seeks a reckoning. The search also leads him to confront God
—apparently the most indifferent and thus the most contemptible
spectator of all. Unfortunately there is no explanation to rescue events
from absurdity. Such an outcome should be sufficient to drive one
mad. But on what terms and in what ways? Thrust into a web of
complicity not of our own choosing, our choices of life—like God's
—are choices of madness whichever way we choose to go. Word from
The Town Beyond the Wall is that this madness is justified and redeemed only when it rebels against forces that choose death. Michael
transmits that message as he does his part to save Pedro from injustice
and as he brings urgency to his own life by working to rescue from
darkness his deranged cellmate, Eliezer ("God has granted my
prayer"). (P. 189)

And what of God?—never far away from the world of this novel
and yet never clearly present either. Is God the silence that is everywhere and nowhere? Or does he live in all aspects of clashing opposites, immovable and yet moving? Neither fully deserving of trust nor
fully able to have people put him aside, his madness prompts two

prayers, leaving us the task to wed them: "Oh God, give me the strength to sin against you, to oppose your will! Give me the strength to deny you, reject you, imprison you, ridicule you!" (P. 53) "Oh God, be with me when I have need of you, but above all do not leave me when I deny you." (P. 49)

Seen from *The Town Beyond the Wall,* what does a cross outside Jerusalem have to say? Its messages stand out best if we recast the characters and scene. Turn the cross into a gallows. Put a number and a Star of David on the victim. Call the executioners SS. See that as victim Jesus is no more—and no less—important than any other "despised and rejected by men." (Isa. 53:3) Recognize that indifference crucifies.

Hold on. Indifference cannot bear that much responsibility. Those who took Jesus's life were passionate not careless. If the Bible is to be believed, God himself willed that Jesus should be "obedient unto death, even death on a cross." (Phil. 2:8) And if SS efficiency kept Germans cool, it can hardly be claimed that death camps emerged from a lack of concern. And yet . . . without indifference would any of these things have been thinkable? Everything permitted in and from the beginning. Too little too late at Calvary—even with an empty tomb and life everlasting promised in the bargain. Too much too soon at Maidanek. The world groans forward in pain that neither God nor humanity cares enough to halt, unless the hands of God or humanity are tied, so that try as anyone may there is no release short of death. Hands tied? Ours? By whom? God's? For what reasons? It doesn't make much sense, however one tries to answer.

But just when the cross makes the least sense, it means the most. That is, if the crucifixion of life, if cries of "My God, my God, why have you forsaken me," cannot and do not rouse us from indifference, can anything? Of course. Everyone could be instantly transformed by some dramatic inbreaking of God's power. After all, with God all things are possible. Quarrels over abstract possibilities avail us little, however, and we do better to learn the lesson of Auschwitz: special dispensations are at best unlikely. So we are back with the old-new challenge: if pain and death are not sufficient to rouse us from indifference, what is?

Nothing, but—such is the next candidate for an answer. In this case the "but" warns that pain and death are numbing, that they are breeders of indifference as well as its products. Too much pain, too much death, equals indifference to both as they become common-place, routine, banal. The Holocaust proves it. Killing became easier and easier, and so it is today. But the numbing effect of pain and death is not the only factor that creates indifference toward them. Another danger is that suffering and death will be too much honored. They will be seen as means to a greater good, as redemptive, as ennobling when they are taken without flinching. For the person who is suffering or dying, convictions of that kind can be a gift to others or a consolation that should not be stripped from anyone who is in circumstances without alternative. Wiesel goes further, however, and links that emphasis to something else. His concern is for the person who can help others and for the responses that such an individual will make.

Instead of meeting needs more pressing than one's own, people too often share views of suffering and dying that should be reserved for those whose plight is greatest. The task for all-who-can, even when they must accept the death of another person, is not to validate suffering but to counteract it, not to legitimate pain but to reduce it, not to sanctify death but to permit it to rob as little of life and integrity as possible. On those counts, Elie Wiesel weighs Christianity and finds it wanting:

> I believe Christians sanctified death because they sanctified the crucifixion. They believed that with that death their religion was born. . . . I believe that one should explore the idea that the sanctification of death throughout the ages produced the indifference to death during the Holocaust.[6]

Wiesel is wrong—on one point. As a religion Christianity began not with a death but with convictions about a resurrection. His assessment is no less important, however, because there can be little doubt that Christianity has a way of changing death, and its attendant suffering, from an enemy into a friend. Indifference to both can result, ironically, from the same source that affirms life by pronouncing its victory over death.

Viewing the cross from *The Town Beyond the Wall,* we Christians should rediscover that Good Friday is not so good. Not for the reason that we deny a transformation of that day from the perspective of Easter, but rather because that triumph should provoke us all the more into determination that human life need not—and therefore must not—be so wasted. When Christians gather around a table to share bread and wine " 'in remembrance of me,' " (1 Cor. 11:23–26) moods of sorrow and repentance, joy and thanksgiving, ought to mix. But they will be hollow feelings unless they are charged by protest, rebellion, and madness over the fact that the one . . . no, that everyone . . . whose body is broken and whose blood is shed is in some sense forsaken without cause or reason. If the sign of the cross is not action that defies the forsaken condition of humanity, it mocks us all.

A method in the madness? Holocaust eyes help us to see the cross as a way of provoking protest against indifference, but still it seems to be such an indirect, inefficient, even counter-productive route to that end. Just for that reason, men and women who follow Jesus after Auschwitz must come to see those facts as causes for protest that can be expressed in no way more authentic than by taking up the cross of Christ anew: not to choose life so that the question, "My God, my God, why have you forsaken me?" is silenced—it can never be—but so the agony and devastation that prompt it are not left to their own devices.

It was another cellmate, Menachem, who suggested to Michael that God puts the question that defies answering: " 'Why does God insist that we come to him by the hardest road?' " (*The Town Beyond the Wall,* p. 146) The Holocaust is one of those paths. It forces Christians to see that the God who wins out over death is the same one who lets it run rampant in the twentieth century. Adequate understandings of that relationship elude us. Nothing but hard options remain: No God . . . Half Gods . . . One God of opposites, tensions, even contradictions. Unless, of course, indifference prevails. Then those options are deadly easy. Harder ways serve better. Keep pursuing a God who refuses to be pinned down. Keep trying to probe questions that defy answers. There is hardly a way to do so short of protest. There is hardly a way to protest well without choosing, healing, righting life as best one can. Results? Such actions make sense where there is none.

By the strange logic of provoking despair until we refuse to despair any longer—Menachem seems to say that such action is involved as we locate a non-resolving resolution to his question. Against despair.

There is a piece of the puzzle, but it is a piece with nothing in the middle. Michael did not know quite what to make of old Menachem. Or better still, Michael does understand him but refuses Menachem's notion that God has " 'taught me only to weep.' " (P. 147) Michael prefers laughter, laughter that signifies resistance. And yet there is no either/or in this situation, not if one recognizes that both laughter and tears can be responses to Menachem's question, responses that are non-accepting acceptances of human fate.

We do not know what happened to Michael. The reader last glimpses him struggling with ebbing strength to bring Eliezer back from the insanity that has left him silent, withdrawn, closed-up. Slowly the boy responds. Michael sees that Pedro's challenge to re-create the universe can occur on an individual, if not a cosmic, level. He talks to Eliezer. The words are beyond his understanding, but Michael is planting seeds. One of them is this: " 'The depth, the meaning, the very salt of man is his constant desire to ask the question ever deeper within himself, to feel ever more intimately the existence of an unknowable answer.' " (P. 187) Probably Michael died in the cell with Eliezer. If so, it is not difficult to imagine his lips forming Paul's words: "We see no answer to our problems, but never despair." (2 Cor. 4:8, The Jerusalem Bible)

As *The Gates of the Forest* opened with a legend, so *The Town Beyond the Wall* closes with another. It tells of a man who suggested to God that the two change places, just for a second. Expressing fear that the man seemed not to share, God nevertheless granted the request. Then, having become God, the man refused to give up his position. The outcome? Unclear, like the fate of Michael and Eliezer, except that Wiesel writes: "As the liberation of the one was bound to the liberation of the other, they renewed the ancient dialogue whose echoes come to us in the night, charged with hatred, with remorse, and most of all, with infinite yearning." (P. 190)

The legend made everything change, and as a result nothing changed for the better. The world was the same or even worse, in spite of and at the same time because of the fact that God and humanity were more mixed up than ever. Duality of good and evil in God and humankind alike—the reversal of roles in the legend portrays that relation and the yearning it produces. Despair seems the order of the day, because the legend intensifies human responsibility. Humankind is given dominion over the earth not only in becoming God, but also insofar as God allows himself to take on human form. The story of the cross is a version of Wiesel's legend, if we can bear it that way. It tells of a God who draws close to humanity for the sake of setting us free. And at least in part that setting-free leaves us—humanity and God alike—forsaken, too.

Why does God insist that we come to him by the hardest way? Elie Wiesel's yearning after the unknowable answer to that question could hardly be stronger. And yet he says more than once that "I never speak of God now. I rather speak of men who believed in God or men who denied God."[7] What can those words mean, especially when they come from one who writes page after page to reveal that "our problem always involves God"?[8] Many factors enter in. A mystical sensitivity precluding the possibility that reason can comprehend and express God's nature. Suspicion that talk about God divides people more than it helps them. Memory of boyhood faith, when only with the greatest care could one be considered worthy to say "God is alive." Refusal to rob that experience of its integrity and thus silence about God now.

There is also apprehension that God is silence, absence, abyss, void, origin and end of all that is but without identity to be clearly grasped and without words for us to hear. And there is also the strategy of the Jewish storyteller: a tradition can be communicated, interpreted, enlivened best not by claims to know what God is or desires, but by relating and sifting what men, women, and children have felt and discerned. Nowhere in this approach is there a repudiation of God's reality. But that reality is also a question, and thus it is clear that "no man can speak on behalf of God."[9] Equally clear is Wiesel's attachment to the idea that we can and should talk *to* God, that much can be learned if we discover how to listen to ourselves, to others who will share their feelings, and even to the silence of God itself.

Not theology so much as sharing. Not theories about life, but choices in its favor. Not elimination of despair, but will against it. Not answers, but questions. Those are messages in *The Town Beyond the Wall.* Hopefully in the lines before your eyes and also in light and shadow that Golgotha and the Holocaust cast on each other.

How Does God Justify Himself in His Own Eyes, Let Alone in Ours?

Not 1933 or 1943. Not even 1948. It is 1967. But Israel is under threat. The death of Jews is still desired. This time, however, there is a difference: the Jews win. The Wall in Jerusalem is recovered, washed with Jewish tears new and old, rebuilt with joy and laughter, even reestablished with prayers. How was victory accomplished? One voice says that " 'Israel won because its army, its people, could deploy six million more names in battle.' "[10] Too much mystification? Perhaps, but memory does count when survival is on the line. Where relations between God and humankind are concerned, memory may count for everything, not merely because it keeps the past present but also because memory colors the future.

Examine how memory works if we move backwards from the resurrection and crucifixion to other factors that contribute decisively to Christian faith. Commandments of God and human sin, for instance. The crucifixion of Jesus occurred because people failed to love (obey) God and neighbor. God suffered in this violation of his will, but did so in a way that shows his love is sufficient to overcome the wrong that men and women do. Living without excuse or justification before God, people are offered a possibility of new life through God's sacrifice of himself, his suffering in our stead, and his own determination that a life of love shall prevail. So goes one version of Christian teaching. It is the tale of "amazing grace"—undeserved, unmerited—that can save a "wretch like me," not so perfection follows but so a clean start is made.

In this Christian account emphasis falls on how persons can be justified before God. Memory focuses on human shortcomings and God's mercy. For centuries, and with a power still felt today, the message of release from sin through faith in Jesus the Christ has touched countless persons. It can continue to do so as long as people sense destructive ways in themselves—and surely no one reading these pages is without that awareness. The memory of such deeds and attitudes haunts us, not simply because of what has already occurred but also because we know that similar acts will crop out viciously again. Confession is not the most popular dimension of Christian worship, but every Christian knows that there is no reconciliation with God apart from it. And thus we offer prayers like this:

> O God, we humbly pray for the forgiveness of the sins named in our own hearts, and for those sins which we share with the whole human family: our lack of trust in you and our self-concern, our prejudice and loyalties misplaced, our failure to care for the earth, the neglect of mercy and justice. And grant that what you so graciously forgive, we in our pride not hold fast, but may leave this place less burdened than when we came; through Jesus Christ our Lord.
> Amen.
> (Taken from a Battell Chapel bulletin, Yale University, dated February 20, 1977)

Thoughts right and true, and no sooner are they uttered than the minister has scripture to assure that we are pardoned. Such grace is not cheap. It makes the full experience of forgiveness depend on "forgiving those who trespass against us," and entails the injunction that we are released to do God's good work in the world. For a moment such a worship experience sets things right between God and an individual, if not the world as a whole. But memory can spoil everything.

Even as a person prays a confession in good faith, complaints may intrude. Humility is no longer simply humble. Reports of failure, indeed of fundamental defects that are exhausted by no recital of particular acts and intentions, turn into questions that ask " 'How does God justify Himself in His own eyes, let alone in ours?' " (*A Beggar in Jerusalem,* p. 38) In turn that question moves toward protest at recognition of the answer: "He doesn't have to." Both question and protest are the result of memory—memory of disaster, tragedy, untimely death, Holocaust. True, our hands have contributed, and if not ours then still the hands of responsibility are human. That fact is the reason for our praying: we cannot undo the past; but by finding release we may move beyond it. Nonetheless there is tension. The God who will supposedly release us and set us off anew is also the One who permits history to scorn itself ever more destructively. Our freedom becomes despair, and where, if anywhere, do such feelings lead? *A Beggar in Jerusalem* points some paths.

The beggar has been in the struggle, and he has seen Jerusalem secured by Israeli troops. God has not thwarted Jewish aims this time around, but the net result still does not add up to satisfaction, for the beggar cannot forget the prices paid—particularly the loss of his friend, Katriel, and the repeated "destructions of Jerusalem elsewhere than in Jerusalem." (P. 82) In joy and sadness the beggar finds companionship with penetrating spirits who gather at the Wall. They are waiting—some for understanding, some for lost friends, and all in their own ways for God. They also swap stories. Two of the beggar's concern commandments, sin and justification.

Jews are marched into a forest. It is hot. Most of the men, women, and children are permitted to sit on the grass while a few dig pits. The job completed, an officer drives up and finds everything in order. He proposes that the action be carried out in family units and lets the people talk things over. Some of the young try to resist, but they are no match for their Nazi guards. The killing is delayed only for a moment. It goes on for hours, interrupted twice. Tevye the Tailor has ten children. It takes time to line them up along the grave. There is also a young man who sings. Apparently the shooting cannot silence him, even though he has no wish to be a lone survivor, a madman whose tale neither can be fully told nor fully heard and believed.

A true story? Yes and no. The scene was not uncommon in days of the *Einsatzgruppen*. Survivors testify that Jewish life continues, even if the particular event described did not occur in fact: after all, "some events do take place but are not true; others are—although they never occurred."[11] As always with Wiesel, however, events portrayed are occasions for speech and silence, and it is in those arenas that the power of his characters and authorship resides. Thus as killers do their work, we hear a Jewish teacher talking to his disciples. For reasons that this man does not know, God " 'demands our lives in sacrifice.' " (*A Beggar in Jerusalem,* p. 86) Very well, they shall accept the inevitable in strength, without asking for mercy that will not be. But the Master adds, " 'Know too that the God of Israel is today violating the Law of Israel. The Torah prohibits killing the cow and her calf on the same day; yet this law, which we have faithfully observed, does not apply to us. See that what is granted to animals is refused to the children of Israel.' " (P. 88)

How does God justify himself in his own eyes, let alone in ours? A giver of commandments who condemns the ones who try most to keep them? What is the sense in that structure for human life? A God who tells people to let justice and mercy flow, but who tolerates conditions that trample the weak and abuse the innocent—isn't it quite clear by now that there is something fundamentally wrong and that human sin and failing are not the whole story? Simply put: God permits too much, and to say that he does so for the sake of freedom, or love, or concern to see the degree to which people can overcome obstacles, or what-have-you, does relatively little to mitigate the horror unleashed in God's on-going relation to the world. Human confessions, right though they are and indispensable for our own health, have a taste of bitterness that only God can change—not by forgiveness but by altering his relationship with human life. Such change seems unlikely. Honesty still dictates that efforts to obey commandments that choose life well should be matched by admissions of failure that seek release to try again. It also dictates that such expressions be forms of protest. Then they include better the passion that enables them to prevail against despair.

Another scene. Katriel is married to Malka, an orphan who wants no children for fear of nourishing death. But Malka is persuaded by Katriel's father, and Sasha is born. The boy is a delight; "then came the day when the parents returned home alone and defeated." (P. 119) Katriel and Malka endured, although at times memory could not be tamed. Once while studying Talmud with his father, Katriel had enough:

> "We love You, God, we fear You, we crown You, we cling to You in spite of You, yet forgive me if I tell You my inner-most thoughts, forgive me for telling You that You are cheating! You give us reason, but You are its limit and its mirror. You command us to be free, but on condition that we make You a gift of that freedom. You order us to love, but You give that love the taste of ashes. You bless us, and You take back Your blessing. Why are You doing all this, to prove what? What truth do You wish to teach us about whom?" (Pp. 119–120)

Not long after, Katriel kissed Malka goodbye and went off to fight for Israel. Malka became an orphan again.

" 'Come now, let us reason together, says the LORD.' " (Isa. 1:18) What follows is God's proclamation of human sins committed, divine decrees to be obeyed with well-being or judgment depending on our choices. Such reasoning turns unreasonable, deceptive, and demonic, given the way life unfolds. Of course, God can reason as he wills. No question on that point. But there are questions about the ways in which he does will to reason, and if we fail to ask them we tend to become consenting victims of the very injustice that we are commanded to forestall and correct. Confession that is only confession, obedience that is only obedience, both leave out a dimension of defiance that God himself may intend for us to bring to bear on him for the sake of combatting despair. A perplexing way to proceed, which may account for silence in the Psalms. One well known portion, for instance, says that "the law of the LORD is perfect, . . . the precepts of the LORD are right, . . . the ordinances of the LORD are true, and righteous altogether." (Ps. 19:7–9) Draw implications as you will, but on the question of whether the Lord himself is righteous, the psalmist does not speak. Today what the biblical writings do *not* say should speak as clearly and profoundly as what they proclaim straight out.

Stop. Aren't all these expressions of defiance too ungracious for a Christian? Aren't they elicited from a perspective that is too Jewish, one that ignores the changed circumstances that the Christian gospel offers? If Jesus has anything to say, it is surely the message that God has our best interests at heart, that he seeks not to condemn the world but to save it, and that God himself provides an ultimate sacrifice for the sake of men and women. So be it, but we've also been through much of this before. That is, God's action in Jesus may be decisive, but it isn't—shouldn't be—all that convincing, even for a Christian. Reason? Too much is still permitted, and because of that fact the accumulation of evil increases, so much so that it becomes incredible to hold that it can be overcome completely. Reason again? The past is what it is. Even if its meaning can be altered by what we remember and forget, short of falsifying the past by erasing apprehension of it, there is no way to move totally beyond it. Things got off to a bad start in the beginning, and they have gone down since. A cross on a hill offers glimmers of hope, some reasons for faith, but it does not halt the descent into hell. The power of God in Christ is less than it is cracked up to be. To decide that it is sufficient to give his only son—or that that is the most that God can do to show his love—such foolishness of God may be just that: foolishness, or worse. Stopping the SS would have been a good supplement, and if Easter accounts of triumph over death are true, surely such intervention in military plans was not beyond the realm of possibility.

The fact that killing went on and on and on is testimony to human sin. But in the interests of clarity, honesty, equity, and even the reconciliation that is so necessary for love's reality, Christians should wonder about the sin of a God who commands us to love. If we do so, one perspective is that the obedience of Jesus unto death, even death on a cross, may be confession on the part of God, an attempt to show that God is atoning for his own sin as much as for that of humankind. But even that twist of incarnation irony would leave things without resolution. The twenty centuries since accentuate God's stubbornness to let things be, far more than his repentance for what they are.

For a long time I was convinced that the Christian has an easier time than the Jew because the Christian believes that the Messiah has come and the Jew is left waiting. Elie Wiesel is one who waits, and speaking of the Messiah, he goes on to add: "One thing is clear to me as a Jew—he hasn't come yet."[12] As I write in this Christian season of Lent, a time of repentance and preparation, I am less sure of my conviction than I was in my pre-Holocaust existence. If I am still prepared to say in any sense that the Messiah has come, I know that such a confession makes—or should make—the Christian's stance even more difficult than the Jew's. Why? Because having claimed that "the Word became flesh and dwelt among us, full of grace and truth," (John 1:14) there is too little grace and truth to be seen. A God who fails to send or to permit the Messiah to appear may be faulted, but not so much as One who sends a Messiah only to let the world unfold too much as if none had been sent at all.

"All of a sudden he seems a changed man. It is hard to tell whether he is blaspheming or preaching faith in the covenant. Impossible to tell whether the anger which moves him is a denial of love or the very opposite: an invocation of love." (*A Beggar in Jerusalem*, pp. 87–88) That description fits the teacher killed by the Nazis. It applies to beggars in Jerusalem. Feel it here, too.

And the reason why traces back to what Christians are commanded to do: " 'You shall love the Lord your God with all your
heart, and with all your soul, and with all your mind. This is the
great and first commandment. And a second is like it, You shall
love your neighbor as yourself.' " (Matt. 22:37–39) Christians
know that those two commandments are related: one loves God
by loving the neighbor, and when the neighbor is loved God is
loved as well. The relation also entails that the neighbor can never
be loved—at least not rightly—at the expense of God. And by the
same token it follows that God must not be loved at the neighbor's expense. Thus, to speak out against God as a way of speaking for one's neighbor can be a way to love God well, provided
the anger carries one into action that serves and heals others. The
right kind of rebellion against God can be our finest service and
love for him. Everything depends on how it works. That dilemma
brings us back to sin, to failures of nerve and courage, to our need
for release from the memories of ourselves, so that we can invoke
love once more.

We spiral around each other—God and humankind. The spiral
itself makes little sense, but inside some features begin to show themselves more clearly. All of us are indicted. All of us are guilty. Nothing
will ever be perfectly right. Nothing justifies anything completely. But
depending on how all of us choose life, we help to justify each other
and thereby find that we can rightly claim some justification in our
own eyes as well. We can only carry out our half of the bargain, acting,
prodding, and serving as best we know, always ready to confess our
faults so as not to be burdened by the chores of self-justification that
do so little to serve other persons. What God shall do remains his
problem—and ours.

A Beggar in Jerusalem ends with the narrator "still here on this
haunted square, in this city where nothing is lost and nothing dis-
persed." (P. 254) But he knows that he will be moving on, homeward
with Malka. There is victory in this story, a small measure of victory.
The cost is staggering, unjustified, perhaps unjustifiable. Better than
no victory at all, though, and enough to suggest that there is sufficient
grace and truth to warrant keeping memory clear, honesty bold, and
service determined as we try to justify our existence and God's by
making both as good as they can be.

Could I Have Been Spared in Kolvillàg So I Could Help a Stranger?

Our itinerary through the major novels of Elie Wiesel has included reflection of the Christian themes of resurrection, the cross, commandment, sin, and justification. An exploration of novels and themes alike suggests that sound reasons for living are found in attitudes of rebellion, protest, and defiance. Destructive elements recognized in God and humanity alike—and most decisively in ourselves—can and therefore must be combatted, but rarely does such struggle produce gains neat and clean. Always the reasons for living are reasons in spite of and against despair. Victories are possible, but in earthly life the Christian can hardly say that he or she has overcome the world, though it may be possible, even indispensable, to be moved by words that John has Jesus speak: " 'In the world you will have trouble, but be brave: I have conquered the world.' " (John 16:33, The Jerusalem Bible)

No one can deny that there is plenty of trouble, nor that courage is essential. Conquering of the world, though, is harder to believe. A journey to Kolvillàg by way of *The Oath* shows why. At the same time it assists Christians to understand the sense that we should give to Jesus's claim. Friendship, which Wiesel calls the dominant theme of this novel, is at the heart of the matter. Friendship: that means putting someone else first, showing compassion, love that is willing to run risks and make sacrifices even unto death—or else its meaning shrinks to nothing at all. Christians sing "What a friend we have in Jesus," and the reason is that we claim Good Friday and Easter to be days that affirm the ultimacy of friendship. But of course it is not that simple.

For one thing we Christians betray the very friendship that lures us. So much so in fact that Wiesel does not miss the target by far with a tale that tells of a conversation between two Jews, one of them an "innocent preacher who had only one word on his lips: love." (*A Beggar in Jerusalem,* p. 67) The other tried to convince him that he ought not to let himself be killed—or at the very least that he ought not to think that his suffering and dying would be redemptive. Misunderstanding and perversion of that message of love would dominate, partly because the message was so simple that it was complex, so straight that it would become obscure in practice. To make this point, the protesting Jew described the horrors that would be visited upon all Jews because of the death of one Jew on a cross. Then it was Jesus's turn to protest back. No, things would not be that way. His heritage would " ' "be a gift of compassion and hope, not a punishment in blood!" ' " (P. 68) Jesus's heart was breaking more than ever. It was too late though—the conversation occurred on Friday. And the outcome? Intended to be a sign of love, too often the cross has become an evil presence.

LOVE: Far from being a solution for the world's troubles, love contributes to them. That idea becomes conceivable when we ask what God was doing in and to the world with Good Friday's cross. But if no solution is provided by love alone, there is none to be had outside of love either. *There is no solution and love must provide it—* that mad paradox confronts the world. *The Oath* explores it by locating friendship against despair.

Azriel (the Lord will help [?]), yet another lone survivor of a holocaust, is past-bound in *The Oath.* His home has been destroyed in a pre-Auschwitz pogrom produced by rumor: the Jews of Kolvillàg have killed a Christian boy in an act of ritual murder.[13] Moshe, eccentric saint of the community, offers himself as guilty of the nonexistent crime. But hate will not be satisfied so easily, and the Jews prepare. Abandoned by their Gentile friends, a few arm themselves. Some celebrate life in the darkness. Most follow age-old wisdom: they rally strength quietly to wait and endure.

The captive Moshe is allowed to speak to his people. By neither word nor deed has Jewish example through the centuries been sufficient to alter inhumanity, nor to persuade God to intervene against senseless killing. So Moshe persuades his people to try a different strategy, to accept an oath of silence. No survivor will reveal anything of what is about to befall Kolvillàg. Only the young Azriel survives. He becomes a wanderer, torn between speech and silence, true to his promise.

Years later, Azriel meets a young man who wishes he were dead. This young person is driven to despair because he is the child of Holocaust survivors. He has no past to match that of his parents, and that of his parents is beyond him. They cannot see him for what he is because they see others—now lost—in him. He cannot locate himself within his family or within the tradition of his people. Azriel decides to intervene, but how to make the young man choose life is the question. Azriel answers by breaking the oath. He tells his tale-which-cannot-be-told, hoping to instill rebellion, responsibility in the place of emptiness, life to counter death.

The young man, and even Azriel, are understandable. The breaking of the oath makes sense, too. But what about Moshe? Was he making sense in calling his people to silence as death stalked them? A hard question. Still, a method in this madness shines through if we follow more of Moshe's thought. Moshe holds that Jews " 'consider death the primary defect and injustice inherent in creation. To die for God is to die against God. For us, man's ultimate confrontation is only with God.' " (*The Oath,* p. 189) Moshe intended the oath as a protest to God and as an offering that might break the hardness of God's heart. He also intended for survivors to use the oath. Life is the prize, not the oath itself, and the oath was taken for the sake of life, especially for the sake of friendship that saves people not " 'from suffering but from indifference to suffering.' " (P. 87)

How could Moshe's oath be used to choose life? By breaking it or by keeping it? Both ways. In either case the oath's power is in its ability to keep one from lethargy and to make one sensitive to acting in ways that count. You cannot keep an oath like Moshe's and fritter life away. Nor can you break such a promise with impunity. Wiesel knows whereof he speaks. "It took me ten years," he says, "to write my first book. It was not a coincidence; it was deliberate. I took a vow of silence in 1945, to the effect that I would wait ten years to be sure that what I would say would be true." ("Talking and Writing and Keeping Silent" in *The German Church Struggle and the Holocaust,* p. 274) He wonders whether it might have been well if all Holocaust survivors had taken an oath of silence and thereby "changed man by the very weight of our silence." (P. 275) He continues:

> But then, I also believe that mankind wouldn't have been able to bear it. It would have driven man and peoples to madness. That is why, I think, we spoke. . . . Somehow the Jew in us is so strong that we believe in communication, we believe in transmission, we believe in sharing. I think the single factor in Jewish existence is this need to communicate. (P. 275)

"Could I have been spared in Kolvillàg so I could help a stranger?" (*The Oath,* p. 32) To Azriel's question comes the answer of friendship: "By allowing me to enter his life, he gave meaning to mine." (P. 16) Moshe . . . Azriel . . . the young man saved from death by a friend. These Jews challenge Christians well. They help us to see the tensions that must be alive in our faith if it is to be good news and not bad. Some of those tensions live in the idea that Christ has overcome the world. We can embrace that promise insofar as it proclaims that the creation is not ultimate, that death is not final, that the forces which pull friends apart shall not work their havoc forever. But such overcoming of the world, we should insist, is in the world only in promises and signs yet to be fulfilled *except* as men, women, and children take up its tasks.

Christians have no exclusive call in this matter, but we are people who are called to be friends to the outcast and downtrodden, the weak and suffering, in the face of warranted despair that finds the world unconquered by love and undone by hatred and indifference. Like that beggar in Jerusalem, we should quarrel with God and even with Jesus about who has done what, when, and where. But even as this disputing sometimes takes the form of words, it must also manifest itself in silent acts which simply do the work that God chose to leave—not merely unfinished but untouched to a degree that keeps despair ever near at hand.

Jesus has overcome the world. It can only begin to be a credible answer if Christians find the claim a question that pushes them to live in ways that emulate the friendship of Jesus—and not so much the friendship found in his dying and rising again, but rather in his *living for* people. Jesus was killed because he lived for people in ways that disturbed oppression, selfishness, exploitation, indifference to crying needs. *Living for* is where the emphasis belongs in this life. Thus, there is a sense in which Christians must keep the Jewish man, Jesus of Nazareth, in tension with the risen Christ of Easter. Not in the sense that one repudiates or contradicts the other. But in the sense that we fail to be true to both unless we protest that the world has not been overcome and give our lives in friendship to defy that fact.

Jesus—God in Christ—has overcome the world? Hard to reconcile that notion with the six million, and they serve as symbols for countless more. Of course Jesus was a victim, too, offered as such by God himself to show that all human sorrow can turn to joy. Such an outlook may work, if we take it on a personal, one-to-one level. Then Jesus is seen as incorporating any destruction, any suffering, that can befall an individual, even the anguish and rage that one should feel in witnessing the suffering of others than oneself. On that basis the sacrifice of God in Christ might be sufficient to overcome every hostility and to achieve reconciliation at every point.

Doubts intrude. The number of victims, the sheer quantity, keeps getting in the way. It makes a disproportion too vast to be balanced, let alone redeemed completely, by the suffering—actual or symbolic —of one Lamb of God. There is the degree of suffering, too. Crucifixion was a brutal way to die, slow and agonizing. But does it stack up to the suffering of individuals at Auschwitz? Even symbolically can we say that Jesus took every form of suffering into himself at Calvary? Did he experience life in a *Sonderkommando,* forced to burn his own family? Or did Jesus become a *Mussulman,* one so starved, exhausted, and sick as to be days dying from the inside out, unable to say anything about it? Could he—could anyone—really have the feelings of a thousand Jewish children waiting their turn, watching their friends consumed by fire at Auschwitz and knowing they would be next? No, for all that Jesus's death is supposed to mean, it was untimely. His suffering passed too easily, too quickly. Proof? He put his protesting question to God only once. Graciously he was given little time to pursue it. His grandeur depends partly on the fact that suffering and death did not take too long. Such lines of thought come to mind after Auschwitz. They help Christians to see that dwelling too much on the passion of Christ can misplace priorities badly.

BUT PAUSE: Isn't the Christian claim one which holds that Christ is a friend who does suffer and die with *Sonderkommandos* and *Mussulmen,* that God's love knows pain wherever and however much it is felt—indeed that Calvary is testimony to that fact just as the open tomb of Easter reveals triumph over suffering and death? Yes . . . and yet is that claim a resolution of anything, or is there a sense in which it actually increases pain and horror, just because so much that did not have to be was suffered unto death? Suffering with and dying with —both are fine when there is nothing more that can be done, when there is no alternative. But the prevention of suffering, putting a stop to it as far as possible—that action is more to the point, and only the suffering that comes from such effort is really justified. God plays it his way. He takes some steps for human well-being, but not all that he can. Thus he prods us to attempt the impossible. So what is the next step?

Echoes of two Christian themes stand out. One is forgiveness, the other God's persuasive love. Difficult to imagine any lasting friendship without the former. It should be sought, urged, practiced without ceasing by humanity and God alike. But once we ask "Who can forgive whom, for what?" the situation is far less simple. One wronged can forgive the wrong done, but not in ways that set everything right, unless we are willing to settle for an unwarranted authority that overlooks actual victims. That is, God can forgive the wrong that I do to him, which may include his identification with human persons I have harmed. But God cannot speak for the human victim. If we think otherwise, we allow God to usurp the victim's prerogative and responsibility. Likewise, if we are convinced that God is implicated deeply in the world's pain, then an individual can forgive the evil from which he goes undelivered, but it is not my place to speak for victims other than myself. To do so is to speak out of turn, to be indifferent to the victim's condition. Emphasis on forgiveness, right as it is, leaves a host of problems.

What about God's persuasive love? Won't it be sufficient to bring everyone around so that the needed circle of forgiveness is completed, so that everything and everybody is made whole once more? Again, the integrity of victims is at stake. Persuasion that forces or alters consciousness against one's will is no persuasion at all. A victory by God on that basis is only deception. All victims may eventually forgive and vindicate God's efforts to persuade. But insofar as memories remain it should come as no surprise if forgiveness is withheld in spite or because of God's involvement with us.

Christians hold that God suffered in Christ. We should also protest that this suffering is not enough, and then make that protest stick by action that checks suffering, even at the price of our own suffering in that attempt. If we extend the range of God's suffering so that we say that God is pained wherever human need goes unmet, then we must still protest that God's suffering counts for too little, and make that protest stick by action that reduces pain, even if—in fact because —we cannot eliminate it. In a word, the Holocaust suggests that Christians must learn from Wiesel's Moshe. We must learn to be for God/against God, for Christ/against Christ, for others/against the tendency toward indifference that lurks in a Christian individualism that regards personal salvation beyond the grave as the end-in-itself.

John has Jesus say, " 'This is my commandment, that you love one another as I have loved you. Greater love has no man than this, that a man lay down his life for his friends. You are my friends if you do what I command you.' " (John 15:12–14) Elie Wiesel writes that Moshe "knew that nothing justifies the pain man causes another. Any messiah in whose name men are tortured can only be a false messiah." (*The Oath,* p. 138) There is a dilemma, permitted by God, that should drive Christians to despair. But what is the next step? To give up? To betray friendship further by denying Jesus, by rejecting God? Or does it wear better to say that the very confusion and hopelessness of our circumstances leave us strangely free to befriend and to love without excuse or apology?

A TRUE STORY: In 1942 a train reached Treblinka. Jews debarked and stripped. Their lives were ending. One member of a Jewish work party recognized a friend in the newly arrived transport and got him assigned to a labor brigade. As the saved man learned what was going on at Treblinka, as he began to suffer his way through the painful work that was keeping him alive, he was not sure that his friend had done him a favor. His doubts were met by this response: " 'I did not save you to keep you alive, but to sell your life at a higher price. You are now a member of a secret organization that is planning an uprising, and you must live.' "[14] An uprising there was, too, even though or because circumstances invited so little hope.

The story provides a model for Christian friendship. We should become not-so-secret members of the body of Christ, rising up in compassion for those most in need. Such a style will not let us rest easy with God, Jesus, or other people, for too much has happened to allow us to take any good for granted. Still, motivated by every energy that refuses to leave people friendless and forsaken, stirred to rebellion because and in spite of the uneasy feeling that we are more alone than we thought at first, we can still—even miraculously—find that we care so much about life that we succeed in checking its self-cancellation. Everyone—Moses, Moshe, Jesus, God, Jews, Christians, humankind, Elie Wiesel, me, you—could then see that bushes burning with friendship need not be consumed. The outcome? More than a small measure of victory against despair.

V
The Last Generation

Search me, O God, and know my heart! Try me and know
my thoughts! And see if there be any wicked way in me,
and lead me in the way everlasting! (Ps. 139:23–24)
And Jesus said, "Father, forgive them; for they know not
what they do." And they cast lots to divide his garments.
(Luke 23:34)
They thought that Auschwitz was possible only because
the world did not know, because the criminals operated in
secret, under cover of night. If the world was silent, it was
only because the world did not know.[1] (Elie Wiesel)

What Supports Them?

There was a time when the last person to see Jesus face to face
lived no longer. Not long after, maybe even within a generation, the
last person to know such an eyewitness also died. Passing from first-
to second-hand, Christian experience became both easier and more
difficult. Reason? Stories touch people as living persons never can,
even as such tales leave doubts in the wonder about what really
happened that trails behind.

Every generation is the last. One day in the years of us now living
there will come an hour when the last eyewitness of the Holocaust is
no longer a survivor. Elie Wiesel fears that moment because it will
make the past easier to forget. So much so that Wiesel once expressed
the additional fear that if the last survivor could be identified, there
would be those who would seek that person's early death so as to make
Auschwitz once-removed. But causes for fear reach still further. In
the lifetime of those born on Sunday afternoon, April 17, 1977, there
will be some unknown person whose fate it is to be the last to know
a Holocaust survivor first-hand.

An insignificant fact? Perhaps. After all, consciousness about the
Holocaust appears to be at a high point, and such concern is generated
just because there is awareness that time and life are passing, tempting

forgetfulness as they go. On the other hand, the capacity of human minds to obscure the past, if not to forget it, is astounding. This generation, like every other, has its revisionist historians. They stand ready to report that the Holocaust is highly exaggerated, even a Zionist fabrication about something that did not occur at all. And some assert that Hitler himself, far from giving orders to initiate the final solution, was actually ignorant of it until very late. Such accounts should suffice to warn us that a Holocaust at second-hand could become no Holocaust at all, and thereby prelude or accompany versions of holocaust-at-first-hand that await future generations or even now take a toll around the earth.

Feelings and questions such as those were mine a week after Passover and Easter as I joined in a Jewish service on Holocaust Remembrance Day *(Yom Hashoah),* and as I witnessed groundbreaking on that day for the New Haven Memorial to the Memory of the Six Million. Reputed to be the first memorial of its kind sponsored by a municipality in the United States, its purpose is to inspire "living proof that the children of New Haven will be taught the meaning of the Memorial, and the terrible history it encompasses."[2] As I contemplated the real significance of the yellow Stars of David that all of us had pinned over our hearts, I was also led to compare the reality that typically compromises such idealism. Usually memorials become so taken for granted as to be void of meaning—or else they are just defaced. And yet? . . . And yet . . . it doesn't have to be that way. Things could be different this time, in spite and because of the fact that the past threatens by receding beyond memory.

Reality proves to be a Holocaust Universe. True, our times are penultimate; life continues to unfold. That unfolding, however, may never eliminate scars that are permanent. Indeed those scars must never be forgotten as Jew and Christian alike face the command to choose life in ways that build and heal beyond them. The edges of reality are ultimately jagged. But how jagged does depend on the future. God is real, man is real, evil and suffering and death are real —just as we experience them to be. What they mean and thus what they become, however, does rest in part with choices yet to be made. Jagged edges are in our hands and in God's. What and how they cut is forever unfinished business.

If a person will discover them by creating, good reasons for choosing life can be found, even in . . . no, especially in a world turned upside down by the Holocaust. Choose life because suffering and indifference are real, because love is possible, and responsibility is put upon us. The truth of these reasons, however, is anything but self-evident. Their validity does not rest on the indubitable foundations of a fully rational universe. They are reasons of refusal, resistance, and rebellion, grounded in and against every power that yields senseless waste. Learn the links between suffering and indifference, between love and responsibility. Respond to suffering with love. Respond to indifference with protest. Such acts will constitute reasons enough to live hard and well.

Elie Wiesel's novels re-echo that basic message. It is not the only theme, however. A counterpoint carries forward from his earlier works; memories, losses, lack of progress in our moral condition continue to gnaw away. Nothing spared the Jews of Kolvillàg. Violence, dances of faith, quiet waiting, reason, madness—none was enough to guarantee that life chosen would be life left to live. Not without cause, then, Wiesel has called *The Oath* his most despairing piece of fiction.[3] Confidence, trust, belief, faith—call it what you will —such a resource must be renewed repeatedly *because it is constantly being lost.* That theme is found again and again in Wiesel's thought, but it is especially accented in a series of writings that should provoke Christians to understand how crucial it is to be *and* not to be our own versions of the last generation.

"The pages that follow are the report of a witness. Nothing more and nothing else. Their purpose is to draw attention to a problem about which no one should remain unaware."[4] *The Jews of Silence* looks straightforward. It reports on the persecution of Russian Jews, and thus tells an old, old tale. The author's aim is to focus the plight of those people, those victims who were among the first to be slaughtered wholesale by Hitler's *Einsatzgruppen* and who are still among the last to be redeemed. Not only is their story difficult to transmit without special messengers. The simplicity of Wiesel's account, sad to say, also turns out not to be simple at all. "If I shall ever be remembered," Elie Wiesel has said, "it will be because of one sentence I coined: The Jews of Silence. Unfortunately, like many other sentences I wrote, this one too was misinterpreted, misunderstood." ("From Holocaust to Rebirth," pp. 10–11)

Usually answers elude this writer, but as Wiesel traveled in the Soviet Union in 1965, he found one that was absolute and clear: the

Jews of Russia really wanted to be Jews. Although under threat to be Jews of *silence,* they were not . . . except for the fact that as they tried to keep their identities intact they could easily wonder whether they lived in a world of silence, devoid of fellow-Jews in blood and/or spirit. Of course, not every Russian Jew expressed a rebellious faith. Fear dominated, and not without reason. Spiritual expressions that occurred on the High Holy Days were all the more remarkable, for the price to be paid in discrimination, hostility, and restricted opportunity could not be taken lightly. By contrast, the most dramatic manifestations of freedom were not in the "free world." Where silence was least necessary, it was most pronounced.

Wiesel found that the Russian Jews did not live in a world of flames. But if "an abyss of blood separates Moscow from Berlin," (*The Jews of Silence,* p. 14) theirs was—no, there is reason enough to put it in the present tense—theirs *is* a Holocaust Universe nonetheless. It is a cold-war world of spiritual destruction, subtle but firm in its reprisals for choices to keep tradition alive, to educate the young, to obey Jewish perception of God's law. It is a world of mistrust and anxiety because enemies are everywhere and nowhere. Betrayers and informers wear no uniforms. They even pose as friends.

No one needs to give up life. The only requirement is to give up Jewishness, although this action will not save a Jew from special passport identification and consequent discrimination. The abject despair of Auschwitz is not so much the problem here, although the factor of isolation links the two places together. Rather there is the hopelessness of seeing a way of life crushed out, not by some killing final solution, but by the terror of being able to live—indeed of being required to do so—under terms set by enemies. And not even God seems to care. That knowledge weights the burden almost beyond belief.

Always careful to qualify his statements by reminders that his sample of Russian Jews may have been too small or too select, Wiesel nonetheless found—to his amazement and even to his shame—that surprising numbers of Russian Jews did choose life on their own terms. Services were held, rituals observed, faith expressed in the face of threats and fears. Supposed Jews of silence were not—are not—so silent after all. Considering the circumstances, Wiesel could honor them by suggesting that "today the only real Jews live in Russia."

(P. 97) Elsewhere, though, indeed whenever destructive suffering is inflicted or permitted with impunity, there is silence in abundance. It knows no boundaries of race or creed, sex or nationality. Listen . . . I can hear it in myself, my profession, my place of work, my church, town, nation. Do your ears hear like mine? Is the sound of silence deafening? And if it is—or isn't—what is the next step?

If Elie Wiesel came away convinced that Russian Jews were committed to being Jewish, there were many other features about them that stayed unclear:

> How they have managed to live by their sacred tradition, without books, without outside help or encouragement, without the hope of a new generation, is a mystery to me. What supports them? How do they overcome the threat of a petrifying rigidity on the one hand and onrushing assimilation on the other? What hidden forces operate among them? It is all a riddle. (P. 45)

It seemed to Wiesel that time might be running out on these people. And if it was doing so for them, it was also fleeting for every man and woman who could lend assistance. Unless help was forthcoming, there would be no one to help. Silence—Jewish or Gentile—outside of the Soviet Union would insure not Jews of silence within, but just silence itself.

What supports them? Answers turn into questions or indictments. God? . . . not in the sense of any obvious deliverance. Faith? . . . not in unswerving conviction that all things will be set right. Defiance of authority? . . . no, fear is too oppressive, too real to permit much in the way of revolutionary aspirations. Loyalty to tradition? . . . yes, like all of the other factors this one figures in despite the negatives, and yet it is insufficient because the meaning of tradition is no longer clear in a setting so alien to everything that tradition affirms. Minority status, shared suffering, will power, determination to survive? . . . important, yes, but just as well they could turn the other way and reinforce Jewish silence, especially when such little encouragement comes from outside.

Move the question closer to home: as Christians, what does or should support us? For those whose experience bears it out, the possibility remains that belief in the God of love, justice, and righteousness as revealed in Jesus of Nazareth is rational, justified, even verified. But if fulfillment of our wishes, hopes, and expectations in this life is the basis for belief, we are on shaky ground indeed. Such ground has always been tenuous, and the abyss of blood that links Berlin and Moscow with New York City and Los Angeles makes it even more so. Individually our lives may turn out well enough, but if we scan the whole human horizon, it is hard to conclude that even a majority of earth's children have fared that way. And if we take our own individual good fortune to be the result of special merit or of special favor from God, the implications of such partiality are morally questionable, if not contrary to Christian teaching.

An alternative view is radically different. It lives in a paradox as strange as faith itself: namely, what can and should support us in our faith is *not* the corroboration of our best expectations *but their frustration.* To bring the point back to *The Jews of Silence,* the faith of Christians can and should find nourishment in the opportunity for service and sharing that human plight and need provide. Indeed if Christian faith does not find its reasons and motivations rooted in the refusal to accept human misery as it comes, its future is dark. It will wither because experience will keep contradicting it, beating down its anticipations for a utopian kingdom of God on earth. It will die when fair turns foul. Better to take the facts of life's destructiveness, the realities of human failure, as sound reason for faith that defies them.

But how does such faith work? For a Christian, it rests on promises—nothing more and nothing less. Promises that love and justice shall prevail, promises that death, the last enemy, has been conquered, promises that the captives shall be liberated, the oppressed set free, and the wrongdoer purged and cleansed so that new life is possible. Promises, promises . . . what are they? . . . deceptive, bogus, valid, sure? If they are good, then for what time and place? No one in his right mind knows the answers to such questions. All that seems certain is that promises like these—whether they are communicated in the traditions of Christianity or Judaism or any other that has such resources—retain a power to attract and win over people from time to time, and not because life shows them to be self-evidently the case but rather because life's destructiveness makes a yearning for their reality so strong as to be irresistible.

The logic here is fragile, delicate—also tough. The former qualities stem from the fact that the very injustice, suffering, waste that create a yearning for something different can be the same factors that make promises incredible. But the toughness mingles in. It lives because human beings prefer good and light and health and honesty at least a little more than evil and darkness and sickness and deceit. And thus promises for the former retain their attraction. True, not everyone will be able to center them in Jesus or even in God, though with respect to God it remains hard to see that there is anything else in reality that could underwrite promises of the magnitude considered here. Certainly human nature, even if it remains tipped in favor of the good, is not capable of making good in the ways required.

For those who do center the promises in Jesus and in God, the very conditions that intensified the yearning for them should be understood as the reasons for faith. Otherwise the faith makes no sense; it would be superfluous, unnecessary. So the question then becomes: what does one do with the promises held in faith? Answer: let them so intensify yearning that the need which blocks their fulfillment is not allowed to stand fast; make them occasions for defying every power—divine and human—that thwarts their coming true. In a word: permit them to grip us with the moral madness portrayed by Elie Wiesel. But pause. What good is all this agitation, especially if we remember that, far from getting better and better, life just goes on and even that much should never be taken for granted? The answer is: who knows? Not the most supportive response, but it does keep open the possibility that some victories can occur. People of faith should not accept that outcome as sufficient, but it should also be sufficient to keep them on the move for now.

And what of last generations? Will there be one of Russian Jews —or just of Jews? Will there be one of Christians? Will there be one of men and women? Again, the answer is: who knows? For that reason every good Christian will pray a Jewish prayer of faith—one which challenges God with its petition even as it makes petition to receive again promises which challenge: "Search me, O God, and know my heart! Try me and know my thoughts! And see if there be any wicked way in me, and lead me in the way everlasting!" (Ps. 139:23–24)

Why Does God Always Act Too Late?

Too late . . . the Holocaust asserts that the question grasps God's actions well—assuming that he involves himself in history at all. And certainly no tenet is more central than the latter as far as Judaism and Christianity are concerned. Precisely there, in fact, is where all the difficulties begin when an event like the Holocaust breaks into the circles of interpretation that those traditions provide. And nowhere are those troubles more intense than when attention dwells on two themes common to both: election and judgment. More stories set the stage.

"And yet, as we listened in silence, with lumps in our throats, it was always of the future that he spoke. The truth was that we needed a future." (*Legends of Our Time,* p. 82) Recollections: a father's death, Yom Kippur in Auschwitz, a meeting with a Spanish Jew, a confrontation with hate. These *Legends of Our Time* deal with the past, but they are about the future, about people—Jewish and Christian—who are taught that they are chosen sons and daughters of God and that there is ultimately a Law and a Judge in the scheme of things. One of these legends is "The Promise." It tells of a Holocaust victim called "the Prophet."

"We loved him," says Elie Wiesel, "because he responded to every appeal for help, he set his face against evil, he clung to his humanity in a world where humanity was denied—and he took very little credit for it." (P. 82) He was a man with his soul set on fire by God's promises, spoken early in covenants with Abraham and Moses, and then in a Messianic spirit to the prophets of Israel. Promises deal with the future, and although the hope that God would keep them—before it was too late—was being killed night by night in Eastern Europe, the Prophet was determined that the future would not die. In Auschwitz that task could be hopeless.

Then a strange thing happened, which shows the thin line between hope and hopelessness, between seizing a future and letting one slip by. The Prophet was pronounced unfit for work; his future was sealed. In that hopelessness, however, energies rallied to save him because he had touched others by living for them. The future was urgent, but also hopeless. There was no reprieve; the Prophet left his friends alone. Not entirely, though. They had been visited, if not by the Messiah himself then by a human spirit that could substitute until something better revealed itself.

The example of a man giving his life for others was enough to give hopeless men a momentary future and even hope for a future in the long run. One difficulty remained: the Prophet was exceptional. He was not Everyone but only One. The Messiah will not come, not altogether, until that relationship is reversed, and yet it may be that "it was its own heart the world incinerated at Auschwitz. . . . Not only man died, but also the idea of man." (P. 230)

Two other stories, shorter this time, and one of them a parable:

> "A man had a fig tree planted in his vineyard; and he came seeking fruit on it and found none. And he said to the vinedresser, 'Lo, these three years I have come seeking fruit on this fig tree, and I find none. Cut it down; why should it use up the ground?' And he answered him, 'Let it alone, sir, this year also, till I dig about it and put on manure. And if it bears fruit next year, well and good; but if not, you can cut it down.' " (Luke 13:6–9)

The storyteller? Jesus of Nazareth . . . a prophet, a person chosen, marked, if ever there was one.

Neither of those stories would ever have been told had it not been for another that preceded them. Many versions exist. Here is one:

> ". . . the LORD your God has chosen you to be a people for his own possession, out of all the peoples that are on the face of the earth. It was not because you were more in number than any other people that the LORD set his love upon you and chose you, for you were the fewest of all peoples; but it is because the LORD loves you, and is keeping the oath which he swore to your fathers, that the LORD has brought you out with a mighty hand, and redeemed you from the house of bondage, from the hand of Pharaoh king of Egypt." (Deut. 7:6–8)

The ending? Unclear, but not likely "they lived happily ever after," for additions kept being made. For example, " 'I will give you as a light to the nations, that my salvation may reach to the end of the earth' " (Isa. 49:6) . . . and then consuming fire seeking to burn that far . . . and then the rebirth of an Israeli nation . . . and then the claim made out of hope and hopelessness: "I believe that our past can save the future. I firmly believe that we Jews can save mankind."[5]

To think of one's people in that way, to identify personally with such a calling—that is really asking for trouble. Events prove it. Not only were the survivors wrong in thinking that the world was silent out of ignorance, but the evidence is also clear that God, if he acts at all, does so far too late. Or is he just confused, misguided, so that he does not know which trees to save and which to cut . . . and perhaps even more importantly when the time is ripe for either act? No, no, surely God knows what he is doing if anyone does. But maybe that *if* assumes too much. It could be that no one does know what is really going on, or that so much is going on that it defies rational comprehension altogether. Either way life would be a good deal simpler than it is if one is committed to the struggles that follow from belief in a God who does know what he is doing and whose relation to the world permits peoples and individuals to feel that their relation to God enjoins special roles and responsibilities.

In a Holocaust Universe is it right to sing "Give me the simple life"? To reflect upon a cold, silent, unfeeling cosmos and to shrug off the Holocaust with a "why did you expect anything different from the absurdity that spawns and lives within us?"—that is one simple way to go. To hold out for other possibilities, other promises, other futures —some of them rooted in sheer defiance against destruction, and some of them doing battle for God/against God—is another. It makes every issue more complicated, every decision harder, every struggle more crucial, every defeat more painful, but not necessarily every victory sweeter because the victories always come too late. Still, only on those terms can the horror of existence be checked from robbing the joy life should contain. Simplicity versus intensity of experience. Tradeoffs move between those poles. Both of them lure and repulse, and with good reason. But after Auschwitz the religious quest that seeks the former and not the latter is one rightly criticized for assuming there is " ' "peace, peace," when there is no peace.' " (Jer. 6:14)

For Christians, no less than for Jews, the most honest—and therefore the best and strongest—appeal they can make to themselves and to others who might join with them is that their way intensifies life, rescuing it from boredom, from mediocrity, from the commonplaces of routine, from indifference or worse. But if Christianity especially is not to fall prey to those same traps, set by self-deceptions from within, it does well to contemplate further what is involved in affirming that "you are a chosen race, a royal priesthood, a holy nation, God's own people." (1 Peter 2:9)

Paul writes that "there is neither Jew nor Greek, there is neither slave nor free, there is neither male nor female; for you are all one in Christ Jesus." (Gal. 3:28) Divisive distinctions of that kind ought to be gone for those who follow Jesus, but Paul's directive can leave standing the idea that Christians are "in" and those outside the fold are "out." What is—should be—the next step? For Christianity, it cannot be a total rejection of the experience that one has been specially called. To serve God by following Jesus is not an inherited or a totally natural role. Some sense of change, redirection, conversion is required. But if those things are true, what needs to occur is that these ideas are tested by Holocaust standards. That is, what does the call to follow Christ mean in a Holocaust Universe? In that perspective, words from Paul stand out again: "Have this mind among yourselves, which you have in Christ Jesus, who, though he was in the form of God, did not count equality with God a thing to be grasped, *but emptied himself, taking the form of a servant,* being born in the likeness of men." (Phil. 2:5–7, my emphasis)

After Auschwitz the only way in which it can make good sense to say that a group or an individual is "chosen" is if that conviction leads men and women to empty themselves in service that meets human need. It is just that simple, and just that difficult. Any other version of this view runs the risk of inflating pride and self-importance. Indeed even being a servant can lead in that direction, particularly if one's role goes unappreciated or is rejected. But the calling itself puts those responses under judgment of their own. Rejected or snubbed, the calling is still that of emptying oneself in service for others. Take it or leave it. No exclusiveness. No smugness. No triumphalism. No guarantees about success on earth are made—except that acceptance of the calling carries with it an intensity of experience that makes life rewarding.

Well, that last provision used to get tagged on, but in a Holocaust Universe it, too, warrants re-examination. Reason?—God always acts too late. Called to serve, as though it would make a difference, the toll of suffering and death continues to mount. The world does not become a better place; it is all that concerned men and women can do to keep it from coming apart completely. Jewish heresy—"there is no Law and no Judge"—is as close to the truth as testimony about God's justice. Who was the vinedresser in the parable told by Jesus? Was it

Jesus pleading out of care for a second chance? Or Satan doing so to assure another round of devastation? Either way God acts too late. True, everything would be different if more people took seriously the Jewish call "to do justice, and to love kindness" (Mic. 6:8) and the Christian call to check need and suffering wherever it is found. The problem of making that urging persuasive, however, is just that the historical odds in its favor are not decisive.

A vicious circle. It must be broken. But how can such breaking best take place? For Jews and Christians one clue is that God calls people to be for God/against God, which is to say that God calls people to be for humanity/against every power that threatens its survival and well-being. A strange calling. Madness. By reaching through and beyond the abundance of death on earth, it elects a person to do combat with the worst that life can offer. To be Jewish or Christian is to hear that appeal. But again, how is the call made? Where is it heard? What are its implications? It is made and heard wherever it is perceived that God acted too late or not at all. It is heard wherever men and women realize that things could have been different, that they did not have to be as they worked out, and where the result is that rebellious determination—Never again!—chooses life. But there is more. For the Jew, the call will not be heard as God's unless rebellious determination includes the challenge that the Law shall be alive within, written on the heart. And for the Christian, the call will not be heard as God's unless rebellious determination manifests itself in one's being a servant of Christ, whose love is alive within, written on the heart.

Why does God always act too late? Answers say too much and too little, but some further questions repay meditation. Could God act too late because he does desire that "justice roll down like waters, and righteousness like an everflowing stream"? (Amos 5:24) Could it be that this desire is present in him precisely because and in spite of the fact that he permits his own will to be divided on the place of justice and righteousness in the scheme of things? Could it be that the yearning within this tension is so strong that God tries to inflame human desire for good by letting things deteriorate toward destruction wherever justice and righteousness are found wanting?

More. Could it be that God's failure to intercede is knowingly a form of judgment that is massively wasteful, unfair, unwarranted?

Could it be that things have now gone so far that the choice is clear: either we rebel against God/for our brothers and sisters, and thus for God, too, by seeking justice and righteousness, or we make the situation worse than before? And could it be the case that even if things have gone so far that there will be no reversal of events on this earth, the choice of life or death remains, only this time with smaller victories at stake (made bigger because they are the ones within our grasp)? If the answer is *yes* in every case, we still do not know why God always acts too late. What we may understand is that life serves God at every turning, and that it is ours to elect not the final outcome but what the quality of our service shall be.

If life serves God at every turning, what follows for God's relation to history? Jews and Christians share belief that God has acted—and therefore may continue to act—in human affairs. In the Exodus, at Sinai, via prophets, and for the Christian through Jesus and the Holy Spirit—in these ways individuals and groups are touched and directed. Neither tradition, however, equates the acts of God with sheer eventuality. The world and human life are a creation in-and-of freedom. God's presence is felt and his voice is heard within them both, but also his absence and silence are real. The independence of creation resides in the latter realities, complicated because such absence and silence give evil its day.

Mostly God lets events run their course. True, there are countless biblical texts that speak of God's doing this-or-that as though men and women are the instruments of his will. Not a few of these instances are scenes of judgment, usually where unfaithfulness on the part of Israel is punished by armed force brought against that people. One may stick with such interpretations if one wishes, seeing the hand of God at work directly in every calamity and catastrophe, in every good and every blessing, or in everything period. *Such outlooks, however, lead to a legitimation of evil that is religiously questionable, morally abhorrent, and deserving of rejection.*

To follow logic that identifies six million Jewish deaths as recompense for sin—scripture may not rule out that interpretation conclusively. But it is enough at variance with biblical priorities—love your neighbor and do nothing to anyone that you would not want done to yourself—that an alternative is enjoined. Better, although far from perfect, to read history as it comes: as the activity of men and women working out their plans and using their powers not as puppets or pawns but as creatures required continually to choose life or death.

The Holocaust, then, is human action, not God's. It is rooted in human judgments, not God's. And if its termination comes only through human intervention and not God's, at least the Holocaust is not legitimated by God's causing it to occur. Men and women bear that responsibility. And yet? . . . And yet . . . it is wrong to take God off the hook entirely. He could have intervened, acted so that the "too little, too late" indictment was less obviously correct. Innocent of directly causing a Holocaust, a verdict that many human persons cannot receive, God still stands trial at Auschwitz. The outcome? Guilty of knowing refusal to stop mass murder when he could have done so.

In spite of God's professed desire for justice, mercy and love, he permits and in that sense does legitimate degrees of their opposites so strong that the children of our children could well be the last generation. And will there be no judgment, no summing up, no setting right when death occurs, seeing that such action will not come plainly on this earth? Or will it? Elie Wiesel, who says that he believes in punishment more than reward, believes also that "one day mankind will have to pay for Auschwitz."[6] God may not need to lift a hand. Human stupidity, callousness, and indifference can be more than enough to condemn us all. But that outcome will sweep away the good and bad with the same indiscriminate waste that has been the problem all along. Will there be nothing more?

One task for persons elected/electing to follow Jesus is to hope and testify that a healing, saving judgment beyond death—if not before—awaits us all, God included. Such judgment will reveal that, like us, God has acted too late. It will not reveal why, but even with that problem hanging on eternally, there is a chance for all of us to confront ourselves and each other with an honesty so expressed that life can be chosen again—this time for the better, if not for the best.

Or would it be easier and simpler just to have one's life returned to dust forever? There's the challenge that wends its way from Elie Wiesel to anyone choosing/chosen to "press on toward the goal for the prize of the upward call of God in Christ Jesus." (Phil. 3:14) Easy ways will not do when there is so much difficulty in living and dying. Simple approaches will not be enough if one heeds voices that cry:

" 'In the wilderness prepare the way of the LORD, make straight in the desert a highway for our God. Every valley shall be lifted up, and every mountain and hill be made low; the uneven ground shall become level, and the rough places a plain.' " (Isa. 40:3–4)

At the end of *Legends of Our Time* there is a "Plea for the Dead." It asks the living not to presume to explain or judge that last generation of Jews killed in the death camps. Too often the victims have been found guilty of their own death through indictments of cowardice, complicity, or tardy response. Such evaluations desecrate. If we seek to understand the victims, that quest must include this judgment: whether these people died in armed resistance, quiet defiance, despairing resignation, or *Mussulman* numbness, they had too few to help them. They had no one on whom to count, except the Nazis. And that judgment cuts even more deeply when this fact is added: their plight was no surprise.

Writing about the men, women, and children in the ghettos and camps who stood and fought the Nazis, Elie Wiesel says, "They were a minority, granted. But is there any society where the active elite is not a minority?" (*Legends of Our Time,* p. 235) Traditions, challenges, problems of election and judgment come together in that Holocaust question. Jews have long been a minority. Today's Christians, even in the United States, are as well. In a world where every generation is potentially the last, can those traditions, or at least some segments within them, take on the role of an active elite whose calling is to empty themselves in saying "never again" to those elements in ourselves and God that invite Holocaust waste? The answer may not be known until-or-because it is too late. Of this much, however, we can be sure: God will not act until it is too late, because he has blessed and judged us—at least for now—with the responsibility/burden of choosing-electing-evaluating life for ourselves.

And Yet, in His Prayers, He Does Not Ask to Be Relieved of His Burden

"As a Jew, you will sooner or later be confronted with the enigma of God's action in history." (*One Generation After,* p. 215)[7] That enigma, we have seen, is the Christian's, too. And there are realms unexplored to which it must still take us. For example, more recollections: dialogues, some snapshots, a watch, a violin, the death of a

teacher, excerpts from a diary and specifically some prayers. These
things form a legacy *One Generation After,* and it underscores a hard
lesson: ultimately there is no explanation. This absence does not
merely reflect the finitude of human reason; it lurks in the ground of
being itself. The Holocaust cannot be understood without God, but
it cannot be understood with him either. The "whys?" are too thick
and too many. Theories based on divine plans, judgment, and punishment for human sin, the idea that some greater good will rise out of
the testing ashes—all of them raise more questions than they satisfy.
It is not that these "explanations" make no sense at all. The difficulty
is that their sense is only partial. Whether freedom or necessity is at
the ground of everything, the outcome is the same. If things could
have worked out differently, why didn't they? If they had to be this
way and no other, why? God can answer by pointing to his will or
by pointing beyond it—to nothing. Can life bear hope in that setting?

The answer "one generation after" is yes—tentatively, defiantly,
imperatively, uncertainly, all at once. But toward what does the
"yes" point? What can be the nature and content of such hope?
Here the humanism in Wiesel's work shines through most clearly.
Thought about God—even rebellion against him—is worthwhile
only to the degree that it kindles desire to choose life well here-and-
now. Obscene, profane—those are evaluations merited by theological reflection and religious practice that do not root moral passion.
So hope cannot be located in God, at any rate not simply, for the
double reason that God is question more than answer. On the one
hand, he refuses to render an accounting to us—either because he
cannot or because he will not. On the other, to be Jewish—also
Christian and human in the best senses—is to hear that silence
shoot back the questions put to God: What are you doing? Are you
choosing life or death?

Hope for a resolution beyond death, a re-creation by God in which
all things are made new—such a prospect does not lure Wiesel very
strongly. It is perhaps too speculative or too much requires an obliter-
ation of the past that would falsify more than is tolerable. So Elie
Wiesel prefers to stick with this world, battered and bruised though
it is. In that situation we can control only what is in our power. That
is both a lot and not much, especially when we consider how little and
badly we manage what is within our authority.

Finding and living with the hope that produces determination to make things better, even though history's record mocks that ideal and suggests that things could get much worse—that is the struggle. For Wiesel, Jews carry forward best by accepting and mastering "our dialectical situation, so Jewishly singular and so singularly Jewish."[8] Their best chance to influence life for the better comes by appropriating all the good that can be found in their tradition. The same lesson applies to Christian men and women. One of its applications points to prayer.

Gospel narratives are full of references to the fact that Jesus was a man of prayer, which is to say that he was thoroughly Jewish. Thus, on one occasion, a disciple—unnamed—said to him, " 'Lord, teach us to pray, as John taught his disciples.' " (Luke 11:1) Interesting to consider who made the request. The practical fisherman, Peter? The more speculative John? Maybe Matthew, the ex-tax collector, or Simon the zealot. Or could it have been the skeptical Thomas or a Judas confused? Whoever—or maybe because of the person who asked, Jesus replied with words that have not been forgotten, even if they have been ignored.

But how does it stand with the Lord's Prayer, or with prayer of any kind, one generation after the Holocaust? Human yearning is so strong that in some form or other prayer is not likely to disappear from the earth. The last generation will still include those who pray. Nonetheless in our own times prayer poses questions: what does it mean to pray for a kingdom to come, for bread, for forgiveness, for resistance to temptation and deliverance from evil—all in a world like this one? Even if we follow Paul's admonition to "pray constantly," (1 Thess. 5:17) will it make any difference? To what degree do responses to the previous questions depend on learning and knowing how to pray after Auschwitz? And can the Holocaust—no less than Jesus himself—teach Christians to pray?

Insofar as prayer is personal/communal sharing with God and other persons, Elie Wiesel's books are a literature of prayer. A good example is "Excerpts from a Diary" in *One Generation After.* The first of these excerpts describes a modest Hasidic house of prayer not far from Wiesel's New York apartment. Survivors go there. One of them, Reb Avraham Zemba, tells how Passover was celebrated with songs in the midst of the Warsaw ghetto uprising, in the midst of deportations to Treblinka. The memory of all that has happened weighs heavily, both in its dimensions of sorrow and in the fervor of a faith that lives on in spite and because of its apparent disconfirmation. "And yet," Wiesel writes of Reb Avraham Zemba, "in his prayers, he does not ask to be relieved of his burden." (*One Generation After,* p. 235) In fact, one point of the excerpt is that this man prays so that he can carry the burden, move it, do something with it so that it becomes not less a burden but more a reason for choosing life well.

If the Holocaust teaches Christians to pray, it does so in the Jewish spirit of Reb Avraham Zemba. Or to put the point more in the words of Jesus, the emphasis must fall on the proposition that " 'if any man would come after me, let him deny himself and take up his cross and follow me.' " (Matt. 16:24) Only with that priority undergirded and encouraged by prayer do other promises take their rightful place: " 'Come to me, all who labor and are heavy laden, and I will give you rest. Take my yoke upon you, and learn from me; for I am gentle and lowly in heart, and you will find rest for your souls. For my yoke is easy, and my burden is light.' " (Matt. 11:28–30) Or, to put the point in the more realistic perspective of Reb Avraham Zemba: " 'The Midrash relates that Rebbe Hanina ben Dossa prayed with such fervor that without being aware of what he was doing, he would pick up a huge stone and carry it elsewhere.' " (*One Generation After,* p. 235)

Can such strength come from prayer, and if so, how? Wiesel's diary does not contain an exhaustive catalog of answers to those questions, but it does offer some clues by way of an example-prayer. It makes seven petitions. None is premised on naive trust in claims such as: " 'Ask, and it will be given you; seek, and you will find; knock, and it will be opened to you. For every one who asks receives, and he who seeks finds, and to him who knocks it will be opened.' " (Matt. 7:7–8) Not that prayer goes unanswered, but just that the answers come in questions, challenges, directives often to be found in a silence that says, "It is up to you. Choose life—well." Our asking God becomes God's asking us. Our seeking is a not-finding that seeks to inflame us in rebellion for the good. Our knocking reveals the awesome openings of One who leaves to our care a world in flames. On this basis, prayer does its work by provoking. At its best it is a method of self-provocation toward service for others, a self-provocation in which God plays a crucial part even if he doesn't know or care about it. But let Wiesel himself teach the rhythm.

> *I no longer ask You for either happiness or paradise; all I ask of You is to listen and let me be aware of Your listening. (One Generation After,* p. 241, my emphasis here and in other prayer excerpts)

Happiness? Paradise? Once upon a time they could be goals for prayer. Now there is too much unhappiness, too much that makes paradise impossible. And *now* is where life struggles to be as best it can. The world is too wild to become fully the kingdom of God announced by Jesus. Result? To pray "Thy Kingdom come on earth as it is in heaven" becomes all the more important as a sign of shared refusal to despair. In that setting it also becomes important to ask fervently that God listen and that he let us be aware of his listening. For our refusal to despair does not mean that it will be successful, does not mean that our burdens will not be crushing.

If God does not listen, or if he chooses not to make his listening felt, the emptiness of prayer can still incite us, although less so than prayer which provokes by awareness that it has been heard. But how does prayer do the latter? By perception of God's direct action in the world or in one's life? In a post-Auschwitz world more likely in awareness that listening is as much as one should expect from God —and in awareness that such listening means more than first appears. For example, where there is listening there can be understanding. Where there is understanding there may be movement rooted in that understanding. Strength to hope could be built. True, there might also be listening without understanding, understanding without movement. Even so prayer can strengthen defiance rooted in a confidence that things do not have to be as they are. Prayer circles itself to ask once more that God should listen and that our being free to struggle on can be received as a sign that we have been heard.

> *I no longer ask You to resolve my questions, only to receive them and make them part of You.* (P. 241)

The issue is usually whether or how prayer is answered. But this particular petition suggests that prayer is best oriented toward questions. Forego asking God to resolve questions and ask instead only that they be received and internalized—that move implies that God can say nothing that will fully satisfy the "whys?" smouldering in Holocaust aftermath. Can such a stance be taken with impunity? When the price of human blood turns every justification into no justification, the petition of prayer should include a plea that questions be allowed to stand and be felt by God as beyond answering. If God's wrath follows, it confirms his irrationality.

No presumption is made as to what the outcome of such divine awareness of questions might be. For all we know, it has been present all along. The main point lies elsewhere: to have God feel the questions as we most profoundly want him to do, then we must feel them ever deeper ourselves. If we keep moving in that direction, then we will find that the questions bounce back to us. The "whys?" put to God become "whys?" put on us. And if we then ask, "What is the next step?" we find that we are pushed out again to do battle with circumstances that produce the questions in the first place. Otherwise our effort to make God feel our questions is hypocritical.

When prayer kindles moral passion, then without our quite knowing it, God may well have felt the questions and underwritten them. Not by answering them, but with determination to let questioning continue. Not so answers will occur farther down the road, but so life can be chosen over death.

> *I no longer ask You for either rest or wisdom, I only ask You not to close me to gratitude, be it of the most trivial kind, or to surprise and friendship. Love? Love is not Yours to give.* (P. 242)

Humble supplication, not to mention an emphasis on God's love —those ingredients are at a premium in Christian understanding of prayer. How could it find a place for such defiance? Meditate like this: the heart of the matter is in asking that whatever has happened, or will happen, one will not be stripped of thanksgiving, not be permitted to become indifferent, and not be rendered incapable of giving or receiving friendship. The request is to be empowered to take up one's cross, not so much with a special infusion of energy that is not there already, but by a releasing of restrictions that thwart our using well what we now possess. Rest and wisdom? They find themselves within these very movements—or not at all.

As for love? Well, if love is not God's to give, since too many opportunities to express it go unrequited, then it must be ours. But pause. That same logic works on us. Missed, lost, broken, forsaken, rejected—that is too much the story of our love. And yet we know that men and women are capable of love, yearn to be loved, need to give love. True of us, can it be different for God? Not if the defiance of Wiesel's prayers holds good, for even if events have become so alien as to make God's love seem unreal, it makes no sense to say that "love is not Yours to give" unless it *is* God's to give. And thus, supported by a petition that asks for openness to surprise, the indictment of God reflects back on us doubly: we must love, and in turn we must be open to receive love, not least from a God whose love appears to be forfeited to evil.

The New Testament teaches that we should "love one another; for love is of God, and he who loves is born of God and knows God. He who does not love does not know God; for God is love." (1 John 4:7–8) God is not only love, any more than we are. Any plain meaning we can give the term so applied to God cannot bear the weight that history puts upon it, unless God is so impotent as to be inconsequential. But in a defiant honesty with ourselves and God as well, especially if tempered by gratitude, surprise, and friendship, there can be a new recognition that love is *everyone's* to give and that the task is for each person to do his or her best to make it real. To the extent that men and women move on that principle, we can discover, too, that God's love for the world is found in his giving us the power to love. That gift is fragile, explosive. It can turn glorious or demonic. What we do goes far in determining which it is. And ironically that point may be driven home to us best by pressing God: What are you doing? Love? Love is not Yours to give. . . . And then we know what tasks are ours, and the Christian learns what it means to take up a cross.

> *As for my enemies, I do not ask You to punish them or even to enlighten them; I only ask You not to lend them Your mask and Your powers. If you must relinquish one or the other, give them Your powers. But not Your countenance.* (P. 242)

A strange appeal here: it would be enough if God kept a greater distance from the world's affairs. For one implication is that life fares badly when he is too close. Again, how could any Christian agree, believing that God became flesh and dwelt among us? And yet that very proclamation should make a Christian wonder, and thus enable identification with this prayer.

Nothing has been more volatile than claims that specify where God is situated, what his affiliations are, where his favor rests. Linked with human proclivity to make such claims exclusive and absolute, the Holocaust is one of their legacies. This prayer, then, provokes self-judgment, self-purification. In asking God to withhold support from powers that turn men and women into enemies—or at least not to permit himself to be identified with those forces—it also warns individuals and communities not to contribute to that same process with their own dogmatic claims. Of course, our keeping God's countenance out of the picture does not solve every problem. God's relation to history—the boundaries of what is permitted and what is not—remains God's problem, or if not problem then still responsibility. But as it makes that fact clear, the prayer shows also that human responsibility for the world is massive.

> *They are modest, my requests, and humble. I ask You what*
> *I might ask a stranger met by chance at twilight in a barren land.*
> (P. 242)

Please listen. Receive my questions. Open me to gratitude, surprise, and friendship. Do not let your full power come too close to us. Yes, correct to say that these prayers are humble simply because they are modest. And yet that is not the whole story either. Modest though they are, these requests ask for a great deal, and not to recognize the taunt that runs through them all is simply self-deception. Modesty and defiance would seem to be poles apart, but the instruction that this prayer imparts is that they can and should be two sides of the same faith. That is, defiance in the face of God already recognizes the difference between Creator and creature, between wills of divine and human proportions. So long, then, as the defiance is not construed as a rejection or denial of God, it cannot be defiance of God without incorporating elements of modesty. By the same token, any humility before God that fails to recognize his capacity to take any protests we can utter does a disservice to the integrity of God and his creatures as well.

But how do these points connect to the image of a stranger met in a barren land at twilight? Many ingredients mix and mingle. Not to presume too much, for example. And yet . . . much would depend on how the stranger was perceived, and on one's condition at twilight in a barren land. Could you help me? Would you help me? Why don't you help me? Why won't you help me? Is that all you can or will do? Questions like those—each one modest, each one defiant, each one both—might be put, and then they might return to us in turn, again with a mixture of modesty and defiance: Give all the help that you can. And what if one is beyond our helping as is the fate of many ravaged souls? Well, there again the combination of modesty and defiance is the right one for faith to have. Human lives too often fall beyond the boundaries of human power to redeem and heal them. What to do with that waste returns to God's doorstep. As it does, another prayer should form our lips, holding God in awe and defiance to this question-promise of despair-defying hope: "If God is for us, who is against us?" (Rom. 8:31)

> *I ask you, God of Abraham, Isaac and Jacob, to enable me to pronounce these words without betraying the child that transmitted them to me: God of Abraham, Isaac and Jacob, enable me to forgive You and enable the child I once was to forgive me too.* (P. 242)

To ask for forgiveness means that things have gone badly wrong, that it would have been better if events had unfolded differently. It is to recognize, too, that even if the past can be overcome it cannot be undone fully. In this prayer, of course, that logic of forgiveness gets a twist. It is not that the one offering the prayer feels no need to be forgiven, but it is true that the prayer is *not* one which asks *God* for that forgiveness. Instead, the one praying seeks forgiveness from himself, and he asks for a healing that will enable *him* to forgive God. Once more prayer cuts against traditional pieties, but for all that it is the more honest. It helps to reveal all that is at stake in the petition to "forgive us our debts, as we also have forgiven our debtors." (Matt. 6:12)

God owes us nothing, that is true. But since we exist without being consulted and in a world not of our own choosing, God gave us the power to hold him responsible as he does us. And so, owing us nothing, God still is our debtor, just as we are his. Wiesel's prayer gets the order right. If our forgiveness comes in proportion to our forgiving of others, then a priority falls on asking for the will to forgive God. Indeed that will power is a prerequisite for genuine forgiveness directed toward other people, and even toward ourselves, and certainly it is true that only if we can forgive ourselves can we fully experience God's forgiveness itself.

Christianity stresses reconciliation, but in a one-sided way. Humanity has erred, not God at all, and the need is for human lives to become contrite and receptive of God's forgiving mercy. The Holocaust teaches a different kind of prayer, one that yields richer reconciliation on a two-way street. Both humanity and God have sinned; each needs forgiveness from the other. Without a spirit of forgiveness toward God, it is hard to keep contact—except in sadness or sorrow over what has been lost—with the childlike innocence, hope, goodness that were known before holocausts intruded. " 'Unless you turn and become like children, you will never enter the kingdom of heaven.' " (Matt. 18:3) Those words of Jesus, now heard after Auschwitz, suggest that a first step is to ask God for power to forgive him so that trust can be built again. To receive that power is also to experience the best forgiveness from God: one that releases us for healing.

> *I no longer ask You for the life of that child, nor even for his faith. I only beg You to listen to him and act in such a way that You and I can listen to him together.* (P. 242)

"For thine is the kingdom, and the power, and the glory forever. Amen."—those words form the right conclusion to Wiesel's final petition. The past cannot return, but it can be felt and heard so that its losses call human hearts beyond sorrow and bitterness toward the determination of "never again." The past may also leave God determined—not bound to transform the world here and now, but resolute that in the end, beyond death, as much love, justice, and mercy as possible, shall prevail. If so, much listening together will be required. Meanwhile, even as "we know that the whole creation has been groaning in travail together until now," (Rom. 8:22; see also Phil. 2:12) we must work out our own salvation in fear and trembling. Such labor means: to listen for and to the best that is within us, to empty ourselves, to take up a cross, to refuse asking to be relieved of our moral burdens, to insure that no generation is made by our hands to be the last.

"Lord, teach us to pray" . . . the Holocaust . . . the prayers of Elie Wiesel's *One Generation After.* A long way—back and forth—from one to the other. And yet not so far, because each speaks to the other, and if Christian and Jew alike will heed wise voices, prayer will work. It will lift a huge stone and carry it elsewhere. Not where it can do no harm, for there is no such place, but at least where it will do less harm than before.

Do You Really Think Man Can Choose to Live?

A doctor's question. More specifically a Russian Jewish doctor's question, posed by a man who is the son of fervent unbelievers, whose wife and child are not Jewish, who is himself not observant, not religious, and yet chooses to belong to a synagogue, seeks to understand what it is to be Jewish. He makes his inquiry between two statements by the old rabbi who is his friend: "You are alive—be grateful for that. To be a Jew means to choose life. . . . It's all a question of where you place the accent. God requires of man not that he live, but that he choose to live. What matters is to choose—at the risk of being defeated."[9]

We have returned to the U.S.S.R. and to madness. Not only the doctor and the rabbi, but also the rabbi's daughter, grandson, and son-in-law, his assistant Zalmen, the chairman of the synagogue, and the rest of a fearful congregation are confronted by choices imposed upon them by an oppressive government intent on forcing silent submission. A troupe of visiting actors from the West (some Jewish, some not) wishes to be with Russian Jews who will recite *Kol Nidre* on Yom Kippur eve.[10] Concerned about appearances, government officials decide to permit the visit, but warnings are issued to the Jews. There must be no disturbances, no protests, nothing to suggest discontent. Almost everyone is willing to go along. However, the old rabbi, provoked by Zalmen, or the madness of God, chooses differently. He breaks silence and testifies to the suffering of his people.

It is a dramatic scene, but nothing much changes—at least on the surface—except that futility gains some ground. The government investigates; Jewish anxiety increases for a time. But no plot is discovered, and fear subsides to a more normal level. The doctor dares the choice of seeking out the visiting actors to drive home the protest made by the rabbi. Unfortunately, they have already gone on their silent way. Although the possibility remains that the rabbi will have a significant relationship with his grandson, his family may be more lost to him than ever, and the madness of his moving protest may have pushed him into disorientation—permanent and useless. Zalmen begins to doubt that his provocation was worth the pain it has caused. Madness compounds itself.

Such is the hopelessness that runs through this drama. Yet hope is intertwined. Slim though its chances, hope directs us to the power of an example, to the courage that makes freedom, to the challenge that says: The rabbi must not be left alone; his sacrifice must not be in vain. Maybe *Zalmen, or the Madness of God* can provoke others to choose well—even at the risk of being defeated. That hope is the premise on which Wiesel's unwritten third act awaits direction by any who will take part in it.

But the complications are massive, and freedom itself is their common root. The old rabbi understands the problems all too well. So often good choices are defeated. They are like seeds described in a parable: As the sower scattered his seeds, they fell in many places, some " 'upon thorns, and the thorns grew up and choked them.' " (Matt. 13:7) (The sower, usually overlooked, is most interesting. He doesn't seem to be very careful about where or how he sows his seed, or maybe he hasn't prepared the ground very well. His sowing leaves the chances for crop failure higher than they need to be. Unless he was just an amateur who didn't know what he was doing. Unlikely that such a sower would have a role in Jesus's tale. No, this sower knows what is going on as he lets events take their own course in freedom. It is not that he is careless, far from that, but that he doesn't do as much as he could to assure a bumper crop. Keeping the sower —or let's be plain about it, keeping God in mind—the words with which Jesus ends the story are well taken: " 'He who has ears, let him hear.' " [13:9]) Still, there is no substitute for sowing if the aim is to get any good return at all, and so the rabbi is correct: the task is to sow and to choose—both as well as possible—even at the risk of being defeated. Nonetheless that right answer will not quiet a nagging "why?"

No one denies that freedom to choose adds significance to life that can come in no other way. To think of ourselves as robot-like, programmed to do everything that we do as though nothing else were really possible—that outlook does not appeal to many persons because it fails to fit the way life feels. Not that there are no lures the other way. Life is easier if we do endorse deterministic theories. Anxiety over responsibility, anguish over what might have been, fear about the possibility that we will misplay the future into self-destruction—all of those concerns are reduced, if not eliminated, by views that call freedom fate. And yet such reduction does not prevail. Freedom's attraction holds.

Highly charged, vast in its potential for evil as well as for good, the freedom given to us is not ours for free. Such realization gives the lie to "explanations" that try to make freedom a sufficient account for the hopelessness of situations like those in *Zalmen* or in a Holocaust. Consider, for example, the following line of thought: the Holocaust occurred because men and women abused the gift of freedom. God is not implicated. As the giver of freedom to choose and act, his gift was wholly good. True, freedom contained a potential for sin, indeed so extensive that it could lead to a Holocaust. But that spectrum was required to open up a range of good uses for freedom which simply could not be without the counterpart of destructive alternatives. If murder were impossible, for instance, the goods of resisting its temptation, of thwarting its actualization, or of moving beyond its waste would no longer be available, not to mention the opportunity afforded God to exercise forgiveness and redemption. Moreover, if one goes on to pose the question of why God does not intervene when suffering reaches Holocaust proportions, the rejoinder is not only that God respects freedom highly but also that its reality—as chosen and given by God—places self-limitations on him. He can't have it both ways: freedom and direct intervention. Freedom gets priority. A Holocaust is permitted.

Related Holocaust "explanations" have been rejected earlier because they apologize for God at the expense of humanity, something which is contrary to the Jewish-Christian conviction that love for one's neighbor is fundamental and the fullest way to love God. That same logic rightly sows seeds of doubt and discord within the analysis of freedom outlined above. To hold that view of freedom as in any way a sufficient justification for human hopelessness is to offer a stone to one who asks for bread. Consider several points in turn to see how.

It makes no sense to say that men and women have not abused the gift of freedom, and that conviction does imply that freedom is a good. But those ideas still leave standing the question of how good freedom is and whether it might have been given better. Viewing the debris of history, it is not difficult to imagine events that life would have been well to do without. I submit: no book, no literary career, no state of Israel, no good that heaven can offer can fully justify the suffering and waste of six million Jewish lives cut off by the Nazis. Adjustments in the nature or use of freedom that would have eliminated such acts would have been far better than what the world got. The Holocaust shows that freedom is not—must not be—the complete answer to our "whys?" Its role is far more to produce them.

Of course God would have had to compromise human freedom to avert the Holocaust. Somewhere human persons would have had to act differently, be checked or moved in ways that did not follow from the natural course of choices actually made. And that is precisely the point: shouldn't God have introduced such compromises, seeing that men and women refused better ways themselves? Wouldn't the tradeoff of less freedom in exchange for less destruction have been worthwhile? Answer as you will. I defend the affirmative. Freedom? Yes. The kind that permits a Holocaust? For the sake of humanity and God alike—No!

Freedom forces encounters with God. What has to be asked boldly is whether God could have intervened and if he could have done so, why he did not act more effectively. Taking the initial part of the issue first, it is important to see that there are more than the two answer-possibilities: yes and no. But stick with the latter—the no—for a moment. To say that God could not intervene would be to picture a God who lacks freedom, one totally at variance with Jewish and Christian scripture, where the emphasis on God's involvement with and power over history is fundamental. In the context of Jewish and Christian faith that option must be set aside. Therefore, yes, God could have intervened, and the third possibility could even be that he was doing so as events unfolded in Berlin, Sighet, Auschwitz, and Washington.

If the third possibility is the right one, then the next question is this: was God doing the most that he could do? Should the answer be yes, we again have a bound God, one whose best efforts were so ineffectual that they seem hardly to have made any difference in the historical situation. Of course it could be argued that things might have been much worse if God had not been at work—whatever that work may have been. There is a point in that assertion, and it should not be overlooked. We do live in a badly distorted world, but it is not the worst state of affairs that could be conceived or made real. Things could and may get much, much worse. Still, that realization does little to mitigate the conviction that they could be much, much better as well.

But wait, say God's apologists. When one holds that God was doing the most he could for the good—as he always does in any situation—the circumstances are much more complicated than the earlier argument assumes. For instance, the world and human actions within it are not atomized events that can be plugged in or changed at random. What we have instead is a set of relationships so detailed, refined, and interconnected that the world's continuity permits only subtle and delicate adjustments by God. Otherwise continuity is radically broken; the world, the place and the status of freedom within it, is dramatically changed. So in terms of intervention, the only way that God can keep a relationship to this particular world, and to particular persons such as we are, is by actions that lure our freedom in one way rather than another but that do not really interfere with our liberty to choose.

Two responses loom large, and as far as the plain meaning of scripture is concerned neither of them can incorporate the notion that God was ignorant, that he did not know what he was doing in creation. First, then, it must be asked: was it necessary for God to create a world leading to a freedom and complexity so great that it effectively curtailed his own ability to intervene decisively enough to prevent a Holocaust? If it was, if there was no other alternative that God could pursue, then it seems we should be honest and say that both Judaism and Christianity are clearly misguided if not simply false. Reason? Both of them, in one way or another, affirm that " 'with God all things are possible.' " (Matt. 19:26)

Rejecting the claim that it was necessary for God to create a world leading to a freedom and complexity such as has now appeared among us, the second question is whether God should have created as he did. Result? Difference of opinion—enough of it honest to make the differences real and lasting. The point here is that if one honestly believes that the world would have been better without some event's occurring, then there is a dispute over what world should have been. Interestingly enough, God himself might make such an evaluation after witnessing all that unfolds—and we should hope that he does so for all our sakes. In any case, it strains credulity to the breaking point to claim that any state of affairs, any total configuration of being, that contains the Holocaust is better than every other one that wouldn't have contained it. To say otherwise is to desert the victims of that event. That act serves no one well. What seems to follow, then, is that God willingly, freely opted for a world that could and did become less good than it or some other might have been.

The next issue is not only "why?" but also to reconsider how it was that God did not intervene more decisively when things got as far out of hand as they did in our Holocaust Universe. Again, making the assumption that a plain reading of scripture enjoins—namely, that he could have done so—the next step is not far to take. God did not want to intervene; at any rate, not enough. And an amplification of that proposition reads as follows: although God did not decree the Holocaust in all its grizzly detail, his commitment to twentieth century life thus far has been one of electing to let human events run their course in freedom-all-too-destructive. Choice. Commitment. Freedom. They form nonsatisfying, nonsatisfactory, nonanswers to the question of why God opted for a world that could become what this one has.

What becomes clear in this analysis is that as one contemplates God's relation to human history, the goodness and innocence of God can be emphasized only at the expense of his power. To the degree that God has, but fails to use, authority that could check destruction like that of the Holocaust, his guilt increases. And if his goodness and innocence are complete, so that he always does the best that he can do in any given set of circumstances, then history itself makes plain that, scripture to the contrary notwithstanding, there is a great deal that is too hard for God.[11] On either count there seems to be no sound basis for trusting the promises that constitute the heart of Jewish and Christian faith alike. Such a situation looks both hopeless and desperate, but in spite or even because of those appearances it may be neither —at least not completely.

Our highest hopes are dashed: things are *not* going to work out for the best. Still, they might work out better instead of worse, and since we know that life can be very, very good—else why the dismay and anger when things turn out otherwise?—then the task is to keep choosing life toward those ends as we can best perceive them. As far as one's relationship to God is concerned, some of the choices include options of the sort just outlined: seeking to encounter a God who is good, innocent, and weak *or* One whose power is really sufficient to transform the world in the end and who therefore stands as guilty for inaction here and now. Short of no God at all and between those two, which one to choose?

The one that best chooses life. But which is that? The Holocaust suggests that we should go with the option which most suggests that "Never again" will stand forever. To the degree that God is weak, that possibility is undermined; to the degree that he is powerful, it has a chance. The chance is there because such a God, even if he persists in a refusal to transform human situations here and now before it is too late, may still empower us to live reformed beyond death. The Holocaust urges the Jew and the Christian to choose for God's power, but in doing so men and women are also choosing the hardest path: the choice is not only for a God when there may be none, but also for a God who may willingly and knowingly defeat us even as we seek him out. In making this choice for life, we are left to be for God/ against God—at the risk of being defeated.

Zalmen, or the Madness of God begins with laughter, the laughter of one not fully normal, not well-adjusted. "Would you like me to tell you a story?" asks Zalmen—of the old rabbi, the audience, or of no one at all except himself (*Zalmen, or the Madness of God*, p. 3). The tale of life-choosing protest unwinds from there . . . all the way to an ending in which more of Zalmen's laughter brings down the curtain on his final words: "And you believed me! You really believed me! That story I just told you . . . it never really happened . . . it couldn't ever have happened. Never! Not here! Not now!" (P. 172) The reader/ viewer is left uncertain about what has been portrayed, what has been claimed and what has not. Was it all in Zalmen's head? Was the telling of the story itself the provocation of the rabbi? Is the technique one of flashback? Is the play somehow all of these at once, or none of them? No matter really. The point of the story comes through on any telling: Be disturbed enough to keep choosing life so that one gives up neither on men and women nor on the power that brought them into being. Zalmen puts it this way: "One has to be mad to believe in God and in man—one has to be mad to believe. One has to be mad today to want to remain human. Be mad, Rabbi, be mad!" (P. 79)

So what about the arguments, analyses, theological ins-and-outs that have occupied these last minutes of your time? Count them as a story, too—fringed with Zalmen-laughter. In imagination's freedom let them in their truth and falsity alike provoke your own life-giving choices: choices that search, try, and know. Choices that forgive what one is entitled to forgive, no more but no less. Choices that uncover the cover of night in which suffering is inflicted, expose that self-deceptive hope which can be the most dangerous of all traps, and defy and break that silence which kills twice by permitting destruction initially and then by demoralizing all who survive. Every generation is the last, but the last can be first. Endings can be beginnings. In their own conflicting and supporting ways, both the Holocaust and the God of a Holocaust Universe tell us that they must be.

VI
Face to Face

"Then I will take away my hand, and you shall see my back; but my face shall not be seen." (Exod. 33:23)

"For the eyes of the Lord are upon the righteous, and his ears are open to their prayer. But the face of the Lord is against those that do evil."[1] (1 Peter 3:12)

His last words were: "At last I shall see Him face to face." We don't know—nor will we ever know—whether these words expressed an ancient fear or a renewed defiance. (Elie Wiesel, *Souls on Fire,* p. 254)

A Resounding Call to Joy

What is a face? Eyes, ears, a mouth and nose, skin smoothed and lined over bones and teeth. Parts of a face, but they do not make one, not alone. Expression—that's closer to the target. Pain and pleasure, laughter and tears, joy and sorrow, kisses and curses, frowns, smiles, fear, anger, love, trust, innocence, guilt. Faces reveal—and hide— who we are. One face with many faces: a fact about everyone. A person lives in each expression, even as none expresses us completely. Faces are important. Not least because I can meet you face to face, but not myself. In such encounters we reveal ourselves to others and thereby to ourselves. What happens then makes all the difference. Meeting face to face honestly, openly, compassionately—or in forgetting, refusing, not caring to do so—people are changed for good or ill.

Something else makes faces crucial. They are images, symbols, that help adults and children to encounter God. The Jewish and Christian traditions protest against idolatry, against all tendencies to elevate creature over Creator. No use of human characteristics, however sophisticated, can describe God fully. But far from voiding speech and imagination, God's transcendence releases both. Biblical writing—whether in the assertion that man is created in God's image, or in the testimony that God speaks through prophets, or in the claim that God entered human flesh—speaks of God as a person. It does so without apology, because experience of him can be communicated in no better way. Thus, God is said to have a face. People live under and with, for and against, its multiple emotions.

What would it be like to meet God face to face? An experience so awesome, so awful, that truly it would kill us? Would we find God's face set against evil? And what would that mean for us—and for God? Would face-to-face encounters with him be occasions for celebration, thanksgiving, rejoicing? Even after Auschwitz? " 'The LORD bless you and keep you: The LORD make his face to shine upon you, and be gracious to you: The LORD lift up his countenance upon you, and give you peace.' " (Num. 6:24–26) Can men and women still receive and extend that benediction?

Three recent books by Elie Wiesel—*Souls on Fire, Ani Maamin,* and *Messengers of God*—reflect on the faces of God. They do so not by speaking about God directly, but rather by telling the stories of Jewish people who heard a benediction and sought to understand and endure its promise. Reason? God may not be discerned face-to-face on this earth, but perhaps his face can be seen indirectly in the faces of human suffering and joy, despair and faith, courage and work.

As these writings nurture a specifically Jewish spirit, they also convey important lessons for Christian conviction that stresses the importance, the goodness, of something like a face-to-face encounter between God and human individuals. Writing to Corinthian Christians, for example, Paul sets out some fundamentals: "For it is the God who said, 'Let light shine out of darkness,' who has shone in our hearts to give the light of the knowledge of the glory of God in the face of Christ." (2 Cor. 4:6) And again: "For now we see in a mirror dimly, but then face to face. Now I know in part; then I shall understand fully, even as I have been fully understood." (1 Cor. 13:12) Meeting faces, those of God and humanity—a richer, more ambiguous, more powerful imagery is hardly to be found. Holocaust experience requires new confrontations with it.

In *Souls on Fire,* Elie Wiesel relates tales of the Hasidim. Many features impress him as he traces this Jewish movement from its flowering in eighteenth century Europe, to its presence in the death camps, and to its surprising influence in a world that came close to exterminating Hasidic ways root and branch. But one of the most important features is that in its highest and best expressions Hasidism is "a resounding call to joy."[2] Generally speaking, the Hasid is a faithful lover of God and thus a person who acts out of love. So there may be Hasidim among the Gentiles as well as among the Jews. More specifically, however, the Hasid is one whose life is informed by the portraits and legends of master teachers who nourished Jewish life in Europe less than three centuries ago. That tradition was decisive in Elie Wiesel's youth; it remains so for him now. Forced to laughter and tears by its past and present, Elie Wiesel carries forward a Hasidic spirit just as other master teachers have done before him: by transmitting tales, commenting on them, offering his own insights, agreeing and disagreeing, questioning and breaking open accumulated experience. He is impelled to do so because he witnessed "that Hasidim remained Hasidim inside the ghetto walls, inside the death camps. In the shadow of the executioner, they celebrated life." (*Souls on Fire* p. 38)

Joy, happiness, thanksgiving—those ingredients make up and call for celebrations. Religiously, at least in American Christianity, celebration is "in." Life is good—let's celebrate. Christ is risen—let's celebrate. God is love—again, let's celebrate. But in the shadow of the executioner? Inside ghetto walls and inside death camps? In the world as we too often find it? Celebrations pall. At any rate they do if taken too simply, too optimistically, without pausing—"And yet . . . and yet"—and without asking "what is going on here?" Can joy, happiness, and thanksgiving be unadulterated in what may be only an interlude between Auschwitz and Hiroshima and destruction that lies in store for all? No doubt such expressions remain possible, but on what terms can they be most honest and authentic? Does the darkness that shadows our lives make celebration, and even worship, more essential than ever?

As Hasidism flourished in Poland, Russia, and other parts of Eastern Europe in the eighteenth and nineteenth centuries, it met a spiritual need among Jews who were victimized by political upheaval and unsatisfied by the competing religious claims of legalism, rationalism, and false messiahs. Imaginative teachers and storytellers, the Hasidic masters of that period blended the old with the new and encouraged spiritual renewal that was humanistic and mystical. It emphasized the sacredness of individual life and a person's responsibility to serve others with compassion. It stressed the necessity and possibility of finding joy in spite of suffering and despair. It urged a fearless desire for honesty and truth. In addition, Hasidism combined a genuine awe of God with direct and emotional reactions toward him. It found God eluding understanding, but also as one to whom people can speak. The Hasidim argued with God, protested against him, feared, trusted, and loved him. All of this was done personally and passionately, without compromising God's majesty and beyond fear of contradiction.

Wiesel's portraits of the Hasidic leaders show admiration for them all. He reveres the teaching of the Baal Shem Tov, decisive early leader of the movement, who believed that God "is at once ally and judge of man inside creation. The bond between them is irreplaceable, it is love. God himself needs love. Whoever loves God will be loved in turn, loved by man and loved by God. It is in man that God must be loved, because the love of God goes through the love of man." (*Souls on Fire,* p. 31) He also prizes the simple joy of Rebbe Zusia, remembered as the "Fool of God" who "simply could not conceive of anything in creation not testifying to God's mercy." (P. 119) But Hasidism was hardly monolithic. Although God's love and mercy were repeated themes, they found their tension and opposition from other Hasidim, if not within their own voices.

Levi-Yitzhak of Berditchev understood his role as that of attorney-for-the-defense, reproaching God for harsh treatment of the Jews. Joining him was one Rebbe Israel, Maggid of Kozhenitz, author of Wiesel's favorite Hasidic prayer: " 'Master of the Universe, know that the children of Israel are suffering too much; they deserve redemption, they need it. But if, for reasons unknown to me, You are not willing, not yet, then redeem all the other nations, but do it soon.' " (P. 133)

Nahman of Bratzlav holds another special place in Wiesel's heart. Laughter is Nahman's gift:

> Laughter that springs from lucid and desperate awareness, a
> mirthless laughter, laughter of protest against the absurdities
> of existence, a laughter of revolt against a universe where man,
> whatever he may do, is condemned in advance. A laughter of

compassion for man who cannot escape the ambiguity of his condition and of his faith. (P. 198)

And a final example, Menahem-Mendl of Kotzk—a spirit whose intense despair yielded righteous anger and revolt so strong that it was said: "a God whose intentions he would understand could not suit him." (P. 245) This rebel embraced life's contradictions both to destroy and to sustain them. Short of death, he found life without release from suffering. At the same time, he affirmed humanity as precious by living defiantly to the end. Wiesel implies, too, that Mendl hoped for something beyond death. His final words were: " 'At last I shall see Him face to face.' " Wiesel adds that "we don't know—nor will we ever know—whether these words expressed an ancient fear or a renewed defiance." (P. 254)

Love, mercy, challenge, irony, laughter, anger, revolt—the Hasidic spirit has them all, but with a difference that transforms. Anything can be said and done, indeed everything *must* be said and done, that is *for* men and women and therefore for God/against God. And it is in that setting, and for those same reasons, that celebration is vital. Wiesel's Hasidim are fiercely humanistic. They affirm life-here-and-now, aim to make it better here-and-now. But this humanism is also predicated on ties to God. Without God, humanity is and can be nothing. The catch—and the challenge—is that even with God humanity may also become nothing. Therefore, life must be lived so that it can be celebrated; it must be celebrated so that it can be lived. Otherwise humanity defeats itself and the goodness of God as well.

Wiesel's Hasidic tales speak of the need to force God's hand. The God in question is no weak idealist who helplessly watches the world run out of control and who cannot respond except by hand-wringing. He is Creator and Master of the Universe. And yet, choosing stubbornly and persistently to be the Creator and Master of *this* universe, ultimate paradoxes emerge: God will not and thus, practically if not logically speaking, cannot move except through the characters he has brought to life to develop and tell his own uncompleted story. This God is different from all of us, yet present in each of us. He has his plan, but it is the plan of freedom working out its own course as individuals and communities live. Therefore, the plan is virtually no plan. It can unleash the worst as well as the best that is in us.

The face of God reflected in Elie Wiesel's portraits of Hasidic

masters is one that listens and answers—usually in the mode of silence. God loves—but by needing our love because he is so often
unlovable in his demands and his harshness, which we encounter
unforgettably, even if sometimes unknowingly. He is ally by being
judge. Judge, not by intervention that metes out justice in obvious
fairness, but by letting events fall as they may to reveal the corruption
and absurdity, as well as the grandeur, of what we do together. The
presence of this God is like the absence of all gods, and therefore
obedience to his will is often found in . . . in what? Rebellion against
it? The logic of the case makes that response a natural candidate, but
like all of the foregoing suggestions about God's face it says too much
and too little. Too much because a focused rebellion is required; too
little because as yet the specific component of celebration is not high-
lighted enough.

A true Hasid always takes the harder path. He lives on the thresh-
old of having things both ways. Not all things, of course, but in
patterns like the following where celebration is concerned: whenever
life is good, it should be celebrated as such. But it can only be celebrated as such to the degree that one realizes how the good stands in
contrast to anything and everything that is worse or better. Celebration is not worthy unless it remembers, incorporates, transforms all
that is unworthy of celebration. And that act, which always runs the
risk of consuming celebration in despair, is in turn unworthy if it loses
any of the joy that was felt originally. The aim is to increase joy, to
multiply reasons and occasions to celebrate. Laughter and tears—
joyous and pained alike. The point is not merely that one can and
should lead to the other, not merely that both should be felt at once,
but that all of these things should occur, spread, and grow, doing so
always in life-affirming ways. Dancing, singing, thanksgiving—all of
these must be forthcoming at every good opportunity, but even more
so when reasons and feelings weigh against them.

This rhythm is difficult to catch. It is not the most natural in the
world, especially in the sadness of a Holocaust Universe. But there is
a logic here, and it is determined to *make* sense of things as far as
human energies are entitled and able to do. Focus on worship-as-
celebration to see some boundaries, especially as they apply to Christian experience rightly sensitized by Hasidic spirit.

Christian worship gives thanks and praise to God. Even if those motives are not primary in any given individual on any given day, all good worship will draw out a genuine expression of thanksgiving from people in attendance. Life provides much that warrants praise, and if there is hurt and sorrow that clouds such first-glance assessments, it is not impossible to cut through to a second level of personal feeling where good reasons for celebration before God are made plain. In either case, though, things complicate quickly.

Celebration that can't sustain itself or persist to the end—religiously speaking neither of those options will do. So, given the world we inhabit, the very causes and experiences of worship celebration must lead us toward, through, and beyond their opposites. If this movement fails, celebration is not necessarily dishonest, but it will be shallow, threatened, unlikely to serve us well or to be of service to others. And the latter ingredient is indispensable. Celebration of one's own good fortune is right and good. But it can mock others who are less favored, and therefore worship violates the command to love one's neighbor as oneself, *unless* its celebration so moves us that we are more committed than ever to the well-being of every brother and sister who can be reached.

But pause. If religious celebration should move us to meet every need that can be reached . . . well, such aims are too large. So won't celebration produce its undoing by pushing all who take it seriously right back into despair over needs that go unmet? Exactly. Given the world we inhabit, how could it be otherwise? But when celebration rightly pushes people in those directions, it can erupt again in faces of protest, rebellion, and defiance—all aimed at conditions, attitudes, actions yielding destruction and suffering that do not have to be. Taking despair into itself in order to combat it, Christian acts of celebration ought to be affirming protests and protesting affirmations rooted in all the reasons there are for saying: "Because of it all, in spite of it all. Thank you, God." (*The Oath,* p. 168)

Paul's advice to Christians includes these admonitions: "Rejoice always, pray constantly, give thanks in all circumstances." (1 Thess. 5:16–18) Such counsel is not far removed from the Hasidic urging to celebrate life, even in the face of executioners. The point, of course, is not to give thanks *for* all circumstances, any more than it is to celebrate life *because* killers kill. Celebration, thanksgiving, worship —these acts are selective just as much as they are deeds for all seasons.

And they have ways of their own to take us beyond their starting points, whether those points are some immediate good fortune or hurt so deep that silence jams every song in our hearts.

"Man's inner liberation," writes Elie Wiesel, "is God's justification." (*Souls on Fire,* p. 111) And Paul, having enjoined us to rejoice, pray, and give thanks, adds that "This is the will of God in Christ Jesus for you." (1 Thess. 5:18) Inner liberation through celebration and vice versa? . . . Is that enough . . . enough to justify God, enough for God to will? No, but those relationships reveal intent in God's face. Life is given to be celebrated. It embodies thanksgiving, or else we endanger life by indifference and make it more absurd than it needs to be. God seems not to bless and keep us as securely as could be wished, nor is his face set against evil as obviously as is desirable. We see too much of God's rear. But for providing men and women with the capacity to celebrate and worship so that we can say anything to God provided it is on behalf of humankind, so that we can check hatred and bitterness by making protest and affirmation one—for those possibilities we should give God praise. Reason? They set us free to try again.

As the Christian calendar moves Sunday by Sunday, as it goes from Christmas through Lent toward Good Friday, Easter, Pentecost and then to Advent once again, varied moods and feelings are accented. Celebration plays more obvious parts in some seasons, but it is never missing from any altogether, and each gives the Christian cause for thanksgiving and worship. As it moves Sabbath by Sabbath, as it goes from the end-and-beginning that Yom Kippur and Rosh Hashanah form together on to Chanukah, Purim, and Passover, the Jewish calendar reflects different experience, but one which also places a premium on celebration, thanksgiving, and worship. Shauvot is a good example. Falling seven weeks after Passover, it commemorates the proclamation of the Ten Commandments on Mount Sinai. More than that, it combines thanksgiving for the Law with celebration for the first fruits of planting. An intriguing combination, because the full harvest of Law and planting lies ahead, promised and even promising, but still unknown because it depends on what nature, humankind, and God will do together.

Still more—Shauvot. As I heard Elie Wiesel explain it on the day itself, he mentioned two other ingredients. It is, he said, a day when

Jews reach out to non-Jews, because the Law was given not to Jews alone but for all people. Moreover, it is a celebration which gives the biblical story of Ruth a prominent part. Ruth was from Moab; she was not originally one of the people of Israel. Twice she married into that covenant. The first time disaster struck and her husband died. Likewise her brother-in-law, and Ruth was left alone with Naomi, her mother-in-law, whose husband had long been dead as well. In spite of Naomi's protest, Ruth stayed with her, and the two women returned to Bethlehem to eke out a living. Times improved when a well-to-do farmer, Boaz, was moved by Ruth's caring for Naomi. He befriended Ruth and married her. Tradition says that their son, Obed, was King David's grandfather. And Christian tradition holds that Jesus came from that line, too.

The point? Two branches—Jewish and Christian—do share a common root. More specifically, just as Ruth affirmed that Naomi's people were her people, and in doing so found good reasons to celebrate, give thanks, and worship, so the Christian can do no better than to appropriate Hasidic qualities of affirming protest and protesting affirmation. But why? Can the point be pushed still further?

For the Christian it all comes back to Jesus and to a dilemma. Christian celebration refers to a Messiah who has been—and is— among us. Right there is the dilemma: it lives in the fact that the world stands unredeemed. True, individual lives have been changed by meeting Jesus—sometimes for the good, though not always. True, Christians have learned to interpret the coming of God's kingdom as an event both postponed and yet promised beyond death. But all of those facts total up to produce a situation in which the Christian needs to be more Hasidic than the Jew. Consider: what circumstances should give greater reason for despair, greater reason for protest, and thus greater reason to celebrate, to give thanks, to worship because of the good that could be and in spite of the evil that is? Believing that there is no Messiah at all? Believing that a Messiah is possible, even waiting for God and humankind together to release him, but that his arrival is not-yet? Or believing that a Messiah has come . . . and finding that so little is different?

Answer for yourself, but encounters with Elie Wiesel convince me that the third choice wins. The way the world turns does not make it difficult to believe that there is no Messiah at all. That view reduces expectations, and thereby diminishes frustration. Such an attitude may already be despairing, but it also avoids hard questions and in that sense is easier. The second option—Jewish—keeps alive the hope that something better is in store. It contends with disappointing postponements, and even with the possibility that hope will be in vain. But neither of these options faces the radical disconfirmation that the Christian position entails: how can a Messiah have come when men and women continue to treat one another so pathetically? For those who believe the Christian claim, this state of affairs should set their souls on fire—in determination that forces of disillusionment shall not have their way.

The Jew's task is to prepare for a Messiah, even to bring him. The Christian's is to show that a Messiah has come. By now the world may have accumulated too much evil to make either task possible. And yet . . . that likelihood is the strongest reason and the best appeal both for being Jewish and for being Christian. The Hasid who celebrates life in the face of the executioner—he or she, Jew or Christian, sees what is at stake, knows that even if earthy battles are lost there is little gained by refusal to defy all that maims. Celebrating life in affirmations that there is a face of God capable of blessing and keeping what is good, both Jew and Christian fight sadness with joy and enable men and women to begin anew.

Is This Your Blessing?

Jacob's question. The same Jacob whose dream revealed a ladder to heaven. The same man who received twin blessings. In one God said that all families of the earth would be blessed by Jacob and his descendants. He should have known there was a catch. Dreamblessings are risky. And yet Jacob counted on them. Still, maybe he wasn't so sure. Biblical editors arranged the tradition about him so that possibility is real: in another night—once more in sleep?—Jacob met a stranger. Man or angel? The text is ambiguous. But there was a struggle. It lasted until dawn, and Jacob seemed to win. His prize? Another blessing: " 'Your name shall no more be called Jacob, but Israel, for you have striven with God and with men, and have prevailed.' " (Gen. 32:28)

There is more. Jacob asked the identity of his adversary and got a question in return: " 'Why is it that you ask my name?' " (Gen. 32:29) Was it in the way that question was asked, or just that his question was answered with a question? Maybe both of those, or neither, but still Jacob felt, heard, and saw enough to believe that he had encountered God. "So Jacob called the name of the place Pení el, saying, 'For I have seen God face to face, and yet my life is preserved.' " (Gen. 32:30)

Pení el (the face of God). Israel (he who strives with God, or God strives). Receiving and giving names like those, Jacob must have kept wondering what to expect. Another of his questions—*Is this your blessing?*—centuries later knows. Where does it come from, this question that answers itself? What is its answer? A poem, Elie Wiesel's *Ani Maamin,* tells that story by using *a song of expectation.* Its theme beckons our attention: where is *encouragement* found for those who choose life by expecting a Messiah who has not come and is therefore too late? How can *courage* be renewed for those who affirm that a Messiah has come even as evidence to the contrary mounts after Auschwitz?

Singing and the strengthening of courage—those two go together. For why do people sing? Because they are happy or blue, carefree or burdened, confident or afraid. They sing to intensify joy already real, to find release from pain by crying out. All these moods and desires need and inspire courage to be. True, one of the best things about singing is that you can do it without thinking, without being philosophical, even without caring. And yet songs can have words and rhythms full of content. They can convey, transmit, and break tradition. They never sound in a vacuum. Rather they move in a matrix of experience, personal and shared, that makes the songs we sing no arbitrary or indifferent matter.

Hopes, fears, feelings—songs live and die with them, and thus it is not far to reach an awareness that songs appeal because they are encouragement. Protest, lament, love, faith, whatever their mood, songs are ways of coping, of celebrating. Of course songs and singing are not always innocent. Both can unleash mad destruction. Both can breed absurdity, carelessness, a courage that is false. The songs we sing, the ways we sing them—both bear watching as we discern how important it is to foster the right kinds of courage.

"O sing to the Lord a new song." Some biblical songs sing that imperative. (For example, see Psalms 33:3, 96:1, and 98:1.) But why a *new* song? Why not an old one, or the same one? The answer isn't clear, though it appears to involve the experience of victory, vindication, blessing for Israel made good. Thus, there is a contrast with other psalms that cry out in lamentation, asking "how long" and pleading for God to heed the people's plight and save them. Although Elie Wiesel's song has more in common with the latter, *Ani Maamin* is also a new song, one sung not only to God but also to men, women, and children. New in a double sense related to the twin blessings received by Jacob: Wiesel's song encourages by attesting to the courageous faith of Jews who have been a blessing to all generations, because of and at the same time in spite of horror-not-of-their-own-choosing. It also encourages by striving to bring human lives face to face with God so that both will strive for each other. *"Ani maamin . . . I believe."* The words continue: *"beviat ha-Mashiah . . . in the coming of the Messiah."* Wiesel calls the song lost-and-found-again. "Both affirmation and provocation," he writes, "it cannot help but evoke uneasiness. And yet . . ."[3] The *uneasiness* is a source of courage. That is one secret of this tale.

In November 1973, Wiesel's song was heard in a cantata version premiered at Carnegie Hall about six weeks after the Yom Kippur War. With music scored by Darius Milhaud, Wiesel's poetic text was based on a song he knew as a boy in Sighet, the words taken from one of Maimonides' thirteen Articles of Faith: "I believe. I believe in the coming of the Messiah, and even if he tarries I shall wait for him on any day that he will come. I believe." It is a long way from Sighet to New York City, and that childhood song has been sung and silenced, lost and found, at many places in between. In Nazi death camps, for example, some Jews found it impossible to sing "Ani maamin"; others found it impossible not to do so. Faith, hope, and courage were lost. They also survived. Wiesel writes proof.

Ani Maamin is a song about a song, but even more it is a plea for singers—muted and released, destroyed and living, human and divine. It focuses on the victims of humanity's darkest hours, but Elie Wiesel speaks to all who survive and therefore need courage to endure and serve. God is included. Wiesel wants people to sing in pain and protest, in remembering, celebrating, and thanksgiving. Although it appears that "the silence of God is God" (*Ani Maamin,* p. 87) or that

"God chooses to be question," (p. 75) he hopes that God's silence includes listening and that God-as-question is not God's only face. In spite of and at the same time because of God's hiddenness, Wiesel longs for him to sing a new song: one of love's triumph over hate, life's victory over death.

"They leave heaven and do not, cannot, see that they are no longer alone: God accompanies them, weeping, smiling, whispering: *Nitzhuni banai,* my children have defeated me, they deserve my gratitude." (P. 105) *Ani Maamin* imagines a meeting between God and three biblical figures: Abraham, Isaac, and Jacob. These patriarchs work to gather "the echoes of Jewish suffering in the world, and make them known in heaven." (P. 15) When history's pain and injustice climax in Nazi slaughter, the observers return from earth to challenge God with Holocaust reports, urging intercession. Undaunted by God's initial silence, the spokesmen tell their story with every skill and emotion they can muster. Defenses for God are not wanting, even or especially in heaven, but the desperate situation of their people inspires courage. Abraham, Isaac, and Jacob refuse to rest content with circumstances that make a mockery of familiar consolation.

Abraham, father of faith and therefore most courageous of men, battles a voice. Unidentified, its identity is clear. Its name? Temptation. Its desire? Acquiescence. Should not people recognize that God acts as he chooses and that their task is to accept his will without question? Abraham resists: God permitted him to plead for Sodom and Gomorrah; nothing less will do when the lives of a million children are at stake. But temptation speaks again: although the ways of God are beyond human understanding, God knows what he is doing. Trust in that understanding must suffice. A second time Abraham demurs: I can see what is happening. Death and dying are everywhere. I agree that the ways of God are beyond understanding. That reality is precisely what cannot, must not be understood.

New strategy by the tempter. Less thunder, fewer threats, more long-range assurance. There is nothing without meaning. Ordeals there are, but God shares them and their outcome is salvation which makes evil cease to be. No, no, no . . . there is too much and too little in this accounting. Too many ordeals, not enough salvation: "What kind of messiah is a messiah who demands six million dead before he reveals himself?" (Pp. 69, 71)

Not much more to say now: God wills, takes, gives back, breaks, consoles . . . that will have to do, have to be enough. But this Abraham is no Job. He will not make Job's response—" 'the LORD gave, and the LORD has taken away; blessed be the name of the LORD' " (Job 1:21)—not yet at any rate. Isaac and Jacob agree. It is too late for consolation. Restoration of an ancient homeland in Israel, a place among nations, Jerusalem recovered—none can make up for what is lost.

Tougher now, the voice. Questions instead of quasi-answers and deceptive consolations: does God owe you an accounting? What have *you* done with creation? God will evade responsibility by holding men and women responsible, even if they are—at least in relative terms—the innocent, just, and faithful.

Which is worse: God's silence or the voice that defends him by temptation? Moot. But in combination they leave the patriarchs without hope. Having tried their best, the best that can be done is to return to their forgotten people. They will tell them the truth that they deserve to know: "God looks on and God is silent." (*Ani Maamin,* p. 83) Such knowledge will not assuage their people's pain, but it may encourage them—in spite of and at the same time because of their hopelessness—to make their dying a revolt, a protest, a repudiation of God's absurd silence.

Slowly the patriarchs retreat from heaven, remembering, experiencing, recounting once more in amazement tales of Jewish belief and courage. They are not recalled. Silence prevails . . . and yet the now unexpected starts to happen. Watch God's face as Abraham witnesses the imminent death of a mother and her children. Abraham snatches a little girl and tries to run her to safety. Too late. But Abraham heard her whisper: "I believe in you." (P. 91) Who is you? Abraham? God? The Messiah? All three. For a child they are inseparable. And Abraham's care for that child is so intense that the tear in God's eye forms unnoticed.

Isaac, too, gets involved in a repetition of his own experience, only this time with no reprieve. The scene: a latter-day Mount Moriah. Not Isaac alone but an entire Jewish community faces a consuming fire. Unexpectedly, the community's judge breaks out in song: "Ani maamin." He knows there will be no Messiah on earth for him. His song is for Isaac's testimony, for God's reprieve, for the world's future. Moved, blessed, pained by what he sees, Isaac also does not, cannot, see God's looking through a veil of tears.

Jacob is looking, too. He sees a man celebrating Passover. The setting? All wrong. The man has no family, no food or drink, no deliverance to celebrate. He will not see Jerusalem next year, for next year he will not be. And yet in this Egypt-without-an-exodus, in this wilderness that knows no law but that of dying, the prophet of promise, Elijah, is invited, expected. A Passover that happened once and that will happen no more is remembered and affirmed. Reason? So that Israel itself will not let Jacob down. So that a people, defended by Jacob, will not let his dreams come to naught through his children's rejection. So that Elijah and God will know the blessing and defiance in a continuing striving with God: "Auschwitz has killed Jews but not their expectation." (P. 103) What Jacob sees also prevents him from encountering the face of God now weeping. God acknowledges defeat. His children deserve gratitude. God begins to move.

The movement is in God's face. It is weeping, smiling, whispering. But to what effect? God's tears are tears of grief, guilt, remorse, compassion, love, and joy all at once. His smile is one of knowing, of admiration, of vindication, of stubborn and harsh determination that good is balanced enough against evil to let men and women continue on their heartbreaking way alone. The whisper says: "What have *I* been doing? What are *you* going to do?" The effect overall? Many emotions become one; it is only God's face that moves. Once more the Messiah is delayed. The unfinished tale of his expected coming will have to move forward, leaving in suspense the question of whether he has been on the way all along.

Other questions remain. Where, for instance, does this song-tale leave Abraham, Isaac, and Jacob? "Heartened by another hope: their children"—that is where. (P. 105) But what does that message mean? Where does it lead? Moreover, what about the stark truth that the patriarchs were going to tell their people? If the patriarchs did not see God's tears, did anyone? And what difference would that make?

Ani Maamin seems to be silent on those points, but not completely. Mutual support and encouragement, a yearning for solidarity, that is what this song is all about. Whether fact or fiction, a tradition of patriarchal intercession gave strength where life was desperate.

And whether fact or fiction, that same strength circled back to nourish the disillusioned Abraham, Isaac, and Jacob. Who is supporting whom? Difficult to answer, although one thing is clear: if the circle is broken anywhere, it is endangered all around. But wait. What is the nature of this support? Doesn't it still rest on the false premise that somehow God cares? Won't, shouldn't, the patriarchs come clean and leave everything in shambles?

That last question—not as easy as it looks. Before it can be handled well another must be posed, one apparently unrelated: what in *Ani Maamin* made God start to cry? Oh, of course, it is only a story and it proves nothing. But then courage is not a matter of proof anyhow. Quite to the contrary, courage makes sense only where there is a lack of proof, and since courage is what we are after, a story about God's tears is not without significance. The trouble is that *Ani Maamin* does not make clear what it was that did bring God to tears. There is no moment when "that's it" and tears begin to flow for one reason alone. The factors are mixed and circular; they are hard to say. One ingredient, however, is surely located in the fact that there are persons, even a people, who live a courageous faith so unjustified and so unwarranted that God can begin to be justified, warranted in the existence he chooses for himself, only if he is moved to tears. Justified? Warranted? True, those categories may be alien to God. The faith that they are not is part of the courage to be in *Ani Maamin.* Who would understand these things better than Abraham, the father of faith, Isaac, who knows that God has the power to kill but also to redeem if he will use it, and Jacob, who became Israel only by refusing to let God go. So . . . what will they do?

Speak truth. But what is that? In this world it is to say that at best God is unlikely to intervene to change events to fit human desire, not even if he weeps over them. Then it is to sing "Ani maamin." It is to say, too, that one factor in God's nonintervention is precisely that same singing. And it is also to say that the alternative—not to sing "Ani maamin"—robs us of courage that must exist to prevent further human deterioration. How does this logic work? What keeps it from dishonesty?

Take the latter question first, and the response is: realism. More than any other century, the twentieth has been one of mass death and mass murder. If not worse than ever before, the world is not better.

The kingdom of God has not come on earth. It is not even breaking in upon us, and it is unreasonable to think that it will. And yet that same realism is a reason both sufficient and necessary for singers of "Ani maamin." Without such singers, realism courts despair too much. It misses opportunities to turn despair against itself. And yet again, to sing "Ani maamin" here-and-now is a "Catch-22." To sing "Ani maamin" in the late twentieth century is to sing out of despair, because of despair, in spite of despair. But as long as "Ani maamin" is sung, despair does not prevail. And where despair does not prevail, God himself does not despair and he lets a world of freedom move along.

A circular scenario. Theater in the round. Absurd. Mad. Yet there is sense to it, a sense that impels us to make all the sense that we can —or else to give up on our children, each other, ourselves. And so not so much for God, but for humankind and in that way for God, "Ani maamin" is one song that must be sung. Not without thinking, not without choosing well the times and places, not without knowing who one's fellow singers are and should be, and not without awareness that even not-singing the song may be on occasion the best way of setting a soul on fire.

Sing "Ani maamin"? But it's a Jewish song, one that disclaims, at least by implication, that Jesus is the Messiah who has already come and who is also here-and-now. How can a Christian sing that song? There are many ways. Not one requires a change in any of the words. "I believe. I believe in the coming of the Messiah, and even if he tarries I shall wait for him on any day that he will come. I believe." Sung Christian-style, "Ani maamin" affirms a coming-already-come. At the same time it incorporates expectation that can agree with the Jew in saying that the coming of Jesus as the Christ is not enough. Jesus comes and tarries . . . promises are made and their fulfillment is postponed . . . God suffers and weeps and both are insufficient. Yearning into the future is no less a Christian experience than it is a quality of Jewishness. Indeed the yearning of the Christian's "Ani maamin" should involve a depth that can make Christians as Jewish as Jews themselves.

Christians share in all the biblical history of the Jews. The difference is that Christians add to that tradition a set of claims and promises that go beyond. Those extra claims and promises are the basis of Christian hope for the future, but they now mix and mingle with worldly experience to create extra burdens and problems, too. Unless Christians violate an essential component of Jesus's teachings and give up on the world, an honest facing of events should make us ask: *because the Messiah has come, in spite of the conviction that the Messiah has come, what are we to do until the Messiah comes?*

As a Christian asks that question, every realistic response forthcoming is fraught with freedom. Not freedom that promises release in deliverance, but rather freedom that delivers us from evil only by challenging us to encounter it in battle. Thus, if Jews sing "Ani maamin" today knowing that there is no Messiah for this earth apart from human effort that makes his coming real, the Christian who sings a version of that song also affirms that the Messiah will tarry just to the extent that Christians fail to be the body of Christ and fail to present their bodies "as a living sacrifice, holy and acceptable." (Rom. 12:1)

Fueled so much by Jesus's question—" 'Who do you say that I am?' " (Matt. 16:15)—Holocaust flames are a refiner's fire (Mal. 3:2): they make plain that all of us now living await redemption. Without the touches, both protesting and healing, that we place upon each other, there will be little evidence of it in our midst. Ruin and rubble are too deep for credibility to hold when Christians argue that it is clear that the Messiah has come, let alone when they advance without protest claims that "there is salvation in no one else" (Acts 4:12) but Jesus. We are free to find nourishment and courage where and when we can, but the Holocaust is a revelation that exclusiveness must reign never again.

When Christians sing "Ani maamin," they should affirm that Jesus is their way, truth, and life, but they should protest from that same stance every view that would read the second part of that pronouncement—" 'no one comes to the Father, but by me' " (John 14:6)—as forming an entrance requirement for admission to the kingdom of God. To sing "Ani maamin" is to sing on behalf of all sorts and conditions of humanity. Not by condoning all that people do but by refusing to give up anyone as lost forever because he or she will make commitments different from one's own. " 'This I command you, to love one another.' " (John 15:17) To obey is to sing "Ani maamin" and vice versa. Taken together, those ingredients affirm the worth of life, care for and hope about its destiny. As they meet needs that cry out desperately, those qualities form the best appeal that Christians can make for other men and women to join them.

Degradation takes such a toll that many people will find sheer foolishness in "Ani maamin." No matter. Or rather all the matter in the world. Just because it is madness to sing "Ani maamin," that is the best reason for singing it, for hearing its call, for joining in a version Jewish, Christian, or what-have-you. And whatever versions are offered and sung, let them do all they can to encourage one another for the sake of defusing Holocaust tendencies. If we do so, Abraham, Isaac, and Jacob, even Jesus, even all of us besieged by a future closing in, up, and out, all of us may be able to see God's tear-stained face. A face that is not deferred beyond death, but that even now, by means of human acts if by no other, is found to bless and keep by lending courage, to shine and be gracious by sparking determination, and to give the peace that can come only in striving well.

Is this your blessing? That "Ani maamin" can still be sung? That it is still possible for men, women, and children to encourage one another? That it is not too late, even after some say the Messiah has come, for the Messiah in us all to move and work in our midst? That God has not withdrawn himself but remains as One worth striving for and against? Could these ideas hold answers? No, not alone. But they are some of the right questions.

Three more make a story that Elie Wiesel likes to tell. When the angel awakens one who has died, inquiries are made: What is your name? How did you use your life? Did you look for redemption? That's all. Quizzing about belief in God is not a top priority, and most assuredly not the Jesus-question, "Who do men say that I am?" True, the questions raised are not unrelated to the latter, but they are less theoretical, more direct. And the answers expected by the angel? I am son of . . . or daughter of. . . . To identify oneself not as an isolated individual, but as a member of a family, a people, a tradition, a cause, a humanity—that is crucial. And then: I tried to serve others. The angel looks for compassion that resists absurdity and indifference. And yes, with the first two answers as context for the third: I did expect more and better life, even against despair.

As Elie Wiesel told the story, he did not elaborate what happens to those who answer well and to those who do not. But that non-ending is because the angel's questions are really questions about courage and blessing *now,* not queries for after-life. Thus, they lend themselves to answering by "Ani maamin."

> "What is your name?"
> *"Singer-of-Ani-Maamin."*
> "How are you using your life?"
> " *'To sing 'Ani maamin.'* "
> "Are you looking for redemption?"
> " *'Ani maamin.'* "

Then What Are You Waiting For? . . . Start Working

Driven from the Garden and apparently rejected by God, Adam and Eve discover paradise lost, shattered bitterly for reasons-without-reason. True, they still have each other, but even that relationship is a mixed blessing. Once the sheer goodness of life had been its own purpose. No more. The purpose of life was now a question. Then something happened: in their anguish not only did they find themselves closer than ever before, but "suddenly they discovered a purpose to their existence: to perfect the world which until then had been no more than created."[4]

Centuries later an ageless dialogue sounded yet again.

> "God, who is perfect, took six days to create a world that is not, how is that possible?"
> "Could you have done better?"
> "Yes, I think so."
> "You could have done better? Then what are you waiting for? You don't have a minute to waste, go ahead, start working!"[5]

Clear enough, those lines. Still, there is confusion. Who speaks? Is the conversation between God and man, and if so who plays which part? Is the dialogue between two people, or is it just carried on in one mind alone? Or is it all of these at once and forever? No matter. All the versions make *work* the issue . . . and it is.

A question for Elie Wiesel: what is work to you? Answer: "Justification. I have to justify every second of my life."[6] Thus we come to *Messengers of God,* a series of biblical portraits and legends that deal with work, with justification, with every second of our lives and

God's. Adam and Eve, Cain and Abel, Abraham and Isaac, Jacob, Joseph, Moses, and Job—telling their stories is the task Wiesel sets for himself in this book. Its premise? "Only today, after the whirlwind of fire and blood that was the Holocaust, do we grasp the full range of implications of the murder of one man by his brother, the deeper meanings of a father's questions and disconcerting silences. Only as we tell them now, in the light of certain experiences of life and death, do we understand them." (*Messengers of God,* pp. xiii-xiv) Strange that Noah is missing, survivor of the Flood, recipient of God's rainbow-promise: never again. But then it must be remembered that Elie Wiesel is a Protestant.

Christians think they have a corner on that category. However, not only is Jewish Protestantism far older, it is often more profound. Discontent merely to affirm God's sovereignty, his disappointment with human life gone wrong, and the importance of grace experienced through faith, a Jewish Protestant gives equal time to other themes: faithfulness must contain allegiance to God that includes disappointment with *his* use of power. Affirmation of the importance of grace must be balanced with honesty that yearns for human well-being and thus for God/against God.

Not without reason, the story of Noah is omitted. Its absence is a protest, for that story is one-sided. God sent the Flood because of his displeasure with men and women. Understandable. But what is not acceptable is that Noah acquiesced. According to the biblical record, no words of protest on behalf of creation came from his lips. He simply followed orders, and one sad result led to another: disappointment with God was doubly warranted. Not only over the sheer waste of the Flood, but because the new world that began with Noah's survival was not new enough. Its foundation was indifference. For that reason, Noah's legend is not to be repeated. Its lesson speaks best in silence. As for those whose stories do appear, their lives are flawed and imperfect, but all are Protestants—Jewish-style.

One thing more about this Jewish Protestantism of Elie Wiesel: it recognizes that God, too, has a Protestant face. Free as he is, God protests that men and women must release the world from bondage to evil, and thereby undo what God himself has permitted. Source of all courage, God protests that we must encourage him not to give up on the world, and that we must do so by making life worth living even when it seems not to be. Claiming that he wants obedience, God breaks his own laws by doing too little, contending in turn that the only workable corrective is for men and women to lodge their own protests through justice and compassion that take obedience one step farther. Wanting reconciliation with humanity, God's seeking of us is so disturbing that it says: be reconciled to me in striving or not at all. Wanting love, God forces debate and defiance to be among its qualities. Hiding his face, he insists that he wants to be known. Aiming at victories, he asserts that the best ones come when he is defeated, when action for God/against God prevails.

Such thinking seems far removed from orthodox Protestantism of a Christian variety. It is too close to blasphemy or to no faith at all. But the point to underscore is that for Elie Wiesel such expressions are not only possible from inside a community of faith; they are indispensable. If God is not seeking rebels to take a stand against misery, absurdity wins hands down. And for a person in a community of faith—Jewish or Christian—that victory is one which neither God nor humanity must be allowed to have. Of course, everything depends on *how* a rebel decides to stand. It is one thing to rebel against God or the teachings of one's tradition as steps in rejecting or denying them. Quite another to do so as the means of pursuing them more profoundly and passionately. Who should understand this better than children of a God-of-protest who "chose what is foolish in the world to shame the wise, . . . chose what is weak in the world to shame the strong, . . . chose what is low and despised in the world, even things that are not, to bring to nothing things that are"? (1 Cor. 1:27–28)

Bound together strangely, with protest-as-love and love-as-protest among the most important links, God and humankind strive for and against each other. According to *Messengers of God,* the worldly task for men and women is monumental: "It is given to man to transform divine injustice into human justice and compassion." (P. 235) Life is not fair. Although the Holocaust escalates that reality, unfairness was also a fact in the beginning. Not in detail perhaps but in outline things were intended that way. Error, deception, and guilt were originally seeds in the Garden of Eden. Bias, favoritism, hurt feelings, vengeance, and murder formed the brotherhood of Cain and Abel. Promises, tests, obedience, trust, survival, hope—these did not make a world of rationality and justice for Abraham and Isaac, but they did create a people.

In the beginning . . . Auschwitz. Jacob fought to secure a blessing, and the world still shakes trying to fathom its nature and portent. Wily Joseph escaped jealous brothers, worked his way to the top, handled Potiphar's wife beautifully, made himself a *Tzaddik,* a Just Man. His success was too much. Unfairly, his people paid the price. Leadership and the law—these associate with Moses. But even this man, closest to God of all, saw only God's backside and had to glimpse the future from so far away that he wondered about the One in charge. That unseen face—was it ugly beyond belief or simply blank, expressionless? Or if not those, then why concealed? Too dazzling, too sublime, too good for a man to see? Not appropriate for a creature to be so familiar with his Creator? Partial reasons. Not enough to satisfy one made to question "why?" nor for God to be self-justified *unless* the question is put to him constantly and his returning silence is found unacceptable. And Job, our contemporary (Jewish or not, who knows?), life had been unfairly good to him. So his testing should be (unfairly?) commensurate?

Wiesel's messengers imply that one face of God is that of unfairness and injustice. It is also a mask that reveals through human rebellion that God elects for us to have hard, impossible, moral work until and through death. What about the face of this God who incites, permits, suffers, endures, and survives a Holocaust Universe? When everything is totaled, does the face belong to friend or foe? The messengers answer: Both . . . and the degree to which it is one or the other largely depends on how we choose to live.

Even now a protest must be entered. Holocaust experiences leave Elie Wiesel suspicious about finding answers to ultimate questions. Answers oversimplify, falsify, settle what is unsettled; they relax tension where it should be felt ever more. He has said:

> I have nothing against questions: they are useful. What is more, they alone are. To turn away from them would be to fail in our duty, to lose our only chance to be able one day to lead an authentic life. It is against the answers that I protest, regardless of their basis. Answers: I say there are none. (*Legends of Our Time,* p. 222)

A hard saying to understand and accept. As for the understanding, Wiesel's protest is not a total rejection of answers to questions. It is directed instead at *explanations,* particularly explanations of the Holocaust that would claim to be authoritative in any final sense.

More specifically, the target is theological explanations of that kind. Short of claims for finality, completeness, obviousness, answers are not so bad or so impossible. We can hardly live without them. But the need and the protest are refusal to rest content with any of them. Answers are made to be probed, tested, found wanting. They exist to be questioned, to be turned into questions that force us beyond. Religiously speaking, such action means to find God in the breaking of encounters in which he seems lost from view, just as it means that in giving our lives for others we find ourselves.

American Christians tend to prefer straightforward claims, problem solutions, non-mystical assurances, meanings plain and simple. The predicament of lacking final answers, of existing without the resolutions we would choose, of acknowledging that uncertainties and questions are the fundamental parts of reality and that life and death really do reflect logics which defy our canons of rationality—those truths are bitter medicine to swallow. And yet medicine they can be: not if our response refuses to recognize them; but hopefully, if we face the abyss and then confess with courage that "we cannot but speak of what we have seen and heard." (Acts 4:20)

In the beginning . . . at the end . . . between: questions, uncertainties. Such conditions are not the demise of religious thought and practice. Far from it. They are the challenge and opportunity that clarify too easily forgotten tasks that both have had all along: "To use the experience. . . . To transmit. To communicate by deed and word. To safeguard. To tell the tale, omitting nothing, forgetting nothing." (*Messengers of God*, p. 28) And for what purposes? Here the answer is straightforward: to liberate and heal, not by settling anything but by caring so that people—and even God—may move each other beyond indifference, sheer numbness, or the giving-up of hope. Americans may continue to ignore or to forget those possibilities, just as recent Holocaust concern may be a passing fad. But if Americans do come to see themselves more and more as situated in a Holocaust Universe, and if we can learn to share the work of *Messengers of God*, then the varieties of our religious experience ought to feel and express an impact that will be no less desirable than it is difficult.

Biblical images, characters, stories, teachings—all have left deep impressions on American life. Adam himself tops the list, for one American dream was that our land would be a New Eden and that its people would be a latter-day-first-born not easily tempted to sin. Only a dream, not half-true. We were more Adam than we knew. In other ways, our problem has been that we were not Adam enough.

"One part of him yearned for God, the other for escape from God." (P. 31) So Elie Wiesel describes Adam's post-fall condition. For many Americans that tension no longer exists. It relaxes in the conclusion that God is dead—or never was—and that we must place our bets on men and women or lose by default. There is truth in that view, although not as neat and simple as might be wished. One difficulty is that America's journey since the early 1960s has been a slide away from optimism toward uncertainty. Political leaders urge doing more with less. Many people try, out of necessity if not by choice, but conviction hangs suspended: will—or can—we come out ahead in facing late twentieth century dilemmas? To the extent that Americans face the Holocaust honestly, they will find the intensity of that question pressing them proportionately.

Driven by Holocaust-consciousness, reaction to the erosion of an optimistic humanism without God takes varied forms. They include: increased cynicism and despair, renewed determination to restore confidence, and even revived yearning for God. Where the latter occurs, however, the need will have a crucial twist too often lacking in most current Christianity. The ways in which Christian communities embrace or reject, meet or refuse it will go far to determine their vitality.

This yearning reinstates the tension Adam felt. It will not be simply the response of a creature acknowledging faults penitentially to a perfect creator and then going on his way rejoicing, born-again. A sense of having been defeated and judged by God may be present, but having tasted the reality of freedom and power, human yearning for God in a post-Holocaust world will also contain anger and rebellion against God for the uses made of his own creative urges. Times of trouble are times of opportunity for religion. After Auschwitz, however, religious life that excuses God without trying him equally will fail to meet and inform raw emotion—feeling that could nourish a revival of a realistic humanism-with-God rooted in acceptance/protest of the fact that "it is given to man to transform divine injustice into human justice and compassion." (*Messengers of God*, p. 235)

A second factor in American religious experience spins out of *Messengers of God:*

> This very ancient story is still our own and we shall continue to be bound to it in the most intimate way. We may not know it, but every one of us, at one time or another, is called upon to play a part in it. What part? Are we Abraham or Isaac? We are Jacob, that is to say, Israel. And Israel began with Abraham. (P. 70)

Americans pledge allegiance to a flag that symbolizes "one nation, under God." Our money reminds us that "in God we trust," and the self-image of a chosen people, a redeemer nation, still influences American behavior. Like Israel's, all of those stories began with Abraham, too.

Although Americans are famous for pioneering the separation of church and state, religion has long been perceived—rightly or wrongly—as one glue that holds our body politic together. Some analyses argue that religion fulfills this function best when it is non-sectarian. There are also laments over the possibility that Americans may be losing a shared faith in a divine providence that watches over our national interest—judging it, to be sure, but protecting it even more so. Because the Holocaust calls God's providence into question on all fronts, an encounter with it will likely erode this *civil religion* further, thus creating needs to re-interpret American visions of God's face. It is questionable whether anything would be gained by a total elimination of civil religion in the United States. More to the point is effort to see whether it can be renewed and used to keep us vigilant and sensitive. Elie Wiesel's reading of Abraham suggests some ways to advance that cause.

Abraham was favored by God. "A man for all seasons, blessed with all talents and virtues, deserving of every grace," he would be the father of a people. (P. 70) Yet the drama of this life centers on an original holocaust: God's commanding test that Abraham should offer his only son, Isaac, as a burnt offering. Such testing was contrary to reason; it was beyond reason, and yet Abraham acted obediently. But the point is that Abraham's obedience was not just obedience— not as Wiesel tells the story. Abraham also tested God to see how far God would go. Abraham won. God relented.

A perverse reversal of the biblical account? Perhaps, but after

Auschwitz, Elie Wiesel urges us to read the Bible with new eyes. Too often God has not relented. For Christians specifically, too many times a promised second coming of Christ—needed even more than it was expected, which is to say quite a lot—has left us empty. Abraham discovered God's guilt, but the greatness of Abraham is in his refusal to give up on God, in his protesting intercession with God for the sake of his people, because and in spite of the hard responsibilities laid upon them. Can American civil religion discern the Jewishness of the old black spiritual and enliven its soul "in the bosom of Abraham"? If it can, if it can recognize the unfairness of life—both in its blessings, which dominate American experience, and in its burdens, which set an agenda of responsibility for us in our dealings with the poor, hungry, and persecuted everywhere—then its vision is worth our trouble. To be true sons and daughters of Abraham ought to be the aim of every face-to-face encounter with God in America.

Moses is a third dimension. "After him," says Wiesel, "nothing was the same again." (*Messengers of God,* p. 181) Life without Moses? Think of it. No Torah. Nothing to set Jews apart from other human groups. No Christianity, no anti-Semitism, and no Holocaust. None of us—not even God. But there is Moses standing before those homeless wanderers, setting before them life and death, urging them to choose well. That Moses, that mad Moshe. He set history's course.

Moses knew God as One who sets people free. He also knew God as a consuming fire, and even as One who "sought to kill him." (Exod. 4:24) Far from Moses's own first choosing, "he filled two equally difficult roles: he was God's emissary to Israel and Israel's to God." (P. 200) For Americans to meet Moses is to keep an appointment with an old friend, for our nation's origins root in visions of Exodus and the establishment of God's New Israel. But how do things work out if that tradition makes contact with a Moses viewing us through Elie Wiesel's Holocaust eyes?

More than one writer suggests that the God of history, not to mention his covenants with human creatures, went up in smoke from Nazi ovens. That conclusion is hard to resist, if we see the faces of God only in terms of traditional notions of full omnipotence and total goodness. At least theoretically, most Americans did learn to view God that way, but Wiesel's Moses never had such illusions. He recognized the sovereignty of God and knew that to confront God was to stand on ground that was holy *but not simply good.* Thus he came to understand that to enter self-consciously into relation with God is to find oneself in a struggle for liberty that requires men and women to contend with God as well as with themselves and each other.

Moses discovered that Gods of history come in many stripes and colors, and what he came to realize is that the One dealing with humanity is a God who cares, but who does so largely by leaving people to sort out a gift of freedom that is at once incredibly vast and wonderful and yet narrow, blind, and destructive. Directives are given and pacts are established as part of the bargain, but they increase the tension more than they dissolve it. Amazing, then, that Moses did not find God a cosmic sadist, a hollow mask of indifference broken only by mocking laughter.

Reasons why? First, Moses saw that people are forgetful, foolish, cowardly—and even worse that they are deceitful, calculating, ready to sell souls for almost any price. And yet the counterpoint was that people could be different. Perfectible? Not likely. But surely less imperfect. Second, an irreplaceable source of courage to struggle for good against evil could come through a sense of covenant with God, so long as it was understood that human service for God required one to be against God, too. Moses, so often pictured as the obedient leader who constantly had to deal with a people stubborn in their rebelliousness, that Moses was actually the most profoundly rebellious of all. Without God, Moses could be nothing. With God, Moses saw ways to bring people to places from which they could at least catch glimpses of a promised land. One religious task, Wiesel's Moses suggests, is to explore whether we can see not the face of a God of history who pulls the strings of events, nor even who uses people as instruments of his own judgment, but rather one whose covenant with a world of freedom requires us to break it in moral rebellion if its goodness is to flourish.

Visions of persuasion and power—further implications for American religious life are focused by hearing Cain speak to God: "I could bring this farce to an end; that may even be what You want, what You are driving me to. But I shall not do it, do You hear me, Master of the Universe, I shall not do it, I shall not destroy, do You hear me, I shall not kill!" (P. 64)[7] And then? Cain did it. He murdered his brother Abel.

Why? The usual interpretation is that Cain was jealous because

Abel's gift to God had been found more acceptable than his. But there is more, at any rate in Elie Wiesel's version. Cain also felt himself tormented by God, pushed by God toward going against God. Not that the going-against would always be wrong, but in this case it would bring needless waste. The only hitch is that neither Cain's awareness nor God's forestalled murder. Deliver us from evil? More than Jesus, Cain may be the first author of that prayer.

Cain's perceptions about divine persuasion rub American optimism the wrong way. God structures the world intentionally so that it may yield madness, violence, brutality of real but unimaginable proportions? News—bad—to us. Those things do occur, but it isn't right to accuse God. It's our fault. We tend to settle for a purely good God or no God at all. It is safer that way, more comforting. But those conclusions resist keeping when Cain is recognized as all-too-contemporary. We would like to buy a portrait of God as "the ideal companion . . . the poet of the world, with tender patience leading it by his vision of truth, beauty, and goodness."[8] We would like to think that God is always doing the best he can. But given the way history unfolds those notions are incredible, at least they are if we also ascribe to God power so extensive and decisive that it can resurrect human individuals from death to everlasting life.

In a Holocaust Universe, a God who is doing the best he can is either not as good as was thought or he is too weak to trust. Thus, what we Americans—especially those of us who are Christian—have to ask religiously is whether we can settle for an innocent but ineffectual God, or whether we must run the risks of relating to a God who is really Master of the Universe but less than perfectly good by any standards we can comprehend. The fragmented, mystical quality of Elie Wiesel's faces of God leaves any final picture clouded, but he inclines toward the second view. True, God's power is limited by virtue of his decision to underwrite human freedom, but this limiting is a self-limitation that God elects in creation, and there is ultimately nothing to necessitate that the decision cannot be modified to permit God's intervention. Moreover, although Wiesel has said that "God does not want man to suffer; man suffers against God," he has also said of his people: "Who didn't persecute us in history? Even God made us suffer."[9]

A God pure but weak, or One who is powerful but of questionable virtue—toward which end of that spectrum should we lean? Is one view more faithful to facts than the other? Does one hold out more hope? We shall have to see. Meanwhile Cain favors the second option. Likewise for Abel.

Too many messages to relate them all. But a final messenger must have his say, for Job is a critical link between Jesus and American Christians. A link of questions.

> Job spoke his outrage, his grief; he told God what He should have known for a long time, perhaps since always, that something was amiss in His universe. The just were punished for no reason, the criminal rewarded for no reason. The just and the wicked were subjected to the same fate—God having turned his back on them, on everyone. God had lost interest in His creation; He was absent. (*Messengers of God,* pp. 229–230)

If Wiesel's Job were here today, how would he respond to the proposition that "Christ is the answer"? Would his car bear a "honk if you love Jesus" bumper sticker? Or in a more sophisticated vein, how would he react to the confession that Jesus reveals a God whose love suffers with us and whose power and victory are in weakness that the world's most killing strength can never overcome? With laughter? Madness? Tears? Would Job's responses be: "Though he slay me, yet will I trust in him. . . . I know that my redeemer liveth"? (Job 13:15 and 19:25, K.J.V.)

Not easy to say. That conclusion is one to draw from Wiesel's interpretation, because he concentrates on Job's final answer to God: "Now, having seen you with my own eyes, I retract all that I have said, and in dust and ashes I repent." (*Messengers of God,* pp. 231–232; Job 42:5–6, The Jerusalem Bible) A simple resignation? Only at first glance. Take another step and Job's answer is resistance and rebellion instead, masked and expressed in hasty abdication. Ultimately, God cannot be defeated. That fact is both our hope and despair, our cause for lamentation and thanksgiving. But in confessing —when God, with greater reason to do so, did not—Job "continued to interrogate God." (P. 235) Of this, therefore, we may be sure: Wiesel's Job would find Jesus a question, whatever the external relationship between them might appear to be.

Although questioning leaves no relationships unchanged, it need not cancel them. Done well, it should push them deeper, make them more profound and lasting. So if Christians agree that all persons "good and bad alike, are in the wrong before God and helpless without his forgiveness," can it suffice after Auschwitz to say that "in Jesus Christ God was reconciling the world to himself" when we see that action simply as the response of divine love to human sinfulness?[10] Or must we Christians also play that theme of reconciliation in variations that include God's sinfulness and human love?

Assuming that Christians speak soundly in referring to "the gravity, cost, and sure achievement of God's reconciling work," must we not also balance the innocence and sacrifice of Holocaust victims against that of God himself, and in doing so see dimensions of gravity and cost—including Christian contributions to anti-Semitism—that render all sure achievements problematic? Or if "God reveals his love in Jesus Christ by showing power in the form of a servant, wisdom in the folly of the cross, and goodness in receiving sinful men," do not Holocaust flames give us pause to re-evaluate the love of love, the power of power, the wisdom of wisdom, and the goodness of goodness?

Christians claim to be on target in saying that Jesus was "the perfect child of God. He was the fulfillment of God's promise to Israel, the beginning of the new creation, and the pioneer of the new humanity. He gave history its meaning and direction and called the church to be his servant for reconciliation of the world. . . . In the power of the risen Christ and the hope of his coming the church sees the promise of God's renewal of man's life in society and of God's victory over all wrong." If we are right in saying those words, then how shall things stand when we transfer to crematoria—real and figurative, past-present-future—words of a Jewish psalmist cried from a cross: "My God, my God, why have you deserted me?" (Ps. 22:1 and Matt. 27:46, The Jerusalem Bible)

The list goes on. Always it leaves the same questions: The Lord bless you and keep you? Make his face to shine upon you? Be gracious to you? Lift up his countenance upon you, and give you peace? The Holocaust . . . Elie Wiesel . . . God . . . face-to-face encounters with those consuming fires test American Christians to make that benediction work. *Can we learn to stand honestly before God, not shirking our responsibilities by blaming him but intensifying our compassion for the world and thereby our love for God—and his for us as well?*

An Epilogue:
Who Is a Jew Today?

Yahweh said to Abram, "Leave your country, your family and your father's house, for the land I will show you. I will make you a great nation; I will bless you and make your name so famous that it will be used as a blessing." (Gen. 12:1–2, The Jerusalem Bible)

"You worship what you do not know; we worship what we know, for salvation is from the Jews." (Jesus of Nazareth, speaking to a Samaritan woman, John 4:22)

The Jew's task has never been to make the world Jewish, but to humanize it. (Elie Wiesel, *A Jew Today,* p. 24, author's translation from French edition)

TIME: 1948–1952. Place: The Soviet Union. Paranoid about a "Jewish conspiracy," Stalin orders death for two hundred Russian Jews: writers, artists, intellectuals. Most are loyal Communists. No matter. They disappear. Even their death is taken from them, for no records exist. And so . . . tests of imagination and truth for an author: what happened to those men and women? what do they teach about being a Jew today?

Those questions are pursued by Elie Wiesel's archetypical survivor. In a novel-in-process one victim escapes Stalin's purge, finds a way to Israel and then back to Russia. Sheer fiction? Perhaps, at least the parts about the survivor and his Russian return. Not the concern, though, nor the insights about threats to life's sanctity and the responses that prod everyone to face the question: who is a Jew today?

A HUNT FOR BURIED TREASURE: A journey to discover what memory has uncovered. Not gold and silver, although they can be found at the location of a second scene. No, this time words are the prize. Words written in haste, under sentence of death that would come one way or the other: too soon or not soon enough. Terse. Painful. Words that say more than sanity allows. Such are the diaries of *Sonderkomman-*

dos. These Jewish prisoners carried corpses to the crematoria. The Nazis reassured them: if you work well, you will live. In fact, within four months most of these *Sonderkommandos* were dead. Beforehand, with whatever they could find and wherever they could do it, they wrote the story of their lives: "Today, August 18, 10 o'clock: I have just buried my wife; 10:15: I have just buried my child."[1]

Elie Wiesel says that this writing is the most powerful he has ever read. He is translating these documents, but the problems are multiple. The Polish government, for instance, is less than eager to let these writings get away. And some have been altered. Wiesel tells of one piece that describes how Hasidic Jews sang in the gas chambers. The "revised" version does not have them singing Jewish hymns, which is thinkable, but the Communist Internationale, which is not.

In the summer of 1977, Wiesel planned to go to Poland to retrieve more *Sonderkommando* diaries and to work on them. Delicate, searing labor—made more so because his trip would take him back to Auschwitz for the first time since 1945. No doubt imagination could produce another diary from that experience. Seeing things familiar made strange by time . . . observing again that the killing installations were of solid construction, intended for permanence . . . glimpsing souvenir stands, Auschwitz as tourist attraction . . . what would such pictures tell this survivor—and us through him—about what it means to be a Jew today? Dangers intervened. There was no trip to Poland. That fact, too, forms a tale about what it *must* mean to be a Jew today.

ANOTHER SCENE: A trial. The defendant is silent. No one will speak for him. Such testing can't go on. It wouldn't be fair. And yet the trial must be held—fairness demands it. Someone in the audience finally steps forward to serve as attorney-for-the-defense. His work is brilliant. Against overwhelming odds, he almost obtains an acquittal. Narrowly, the verdict comes in: guilty-as-charged. The charge? Any number of things. You see, the defendant is God, and the situation is an unrelenting slaughter of innocence. And the defense attorney? Words made flesh in Satan himself.

Sheer fiction again? Yes and no. Elie Wiesel reports that he did witness a trial of God at Auschwitz. That scene has stayed with him for years, and he has tried in varied ways to put it into words. He thinks he has the format now: a drama set at the turn of the century. It will ask: why should one be a Jew today?

WORKS-IN-PROCESS: Elie Wiesel always has something under way. Not just books either. He travels far and wide, speaks to audiences all over the world, teaches students. In his special way he is a moral prophet and a political activist. With time's passage, urgency about his work increases. Reason? The farther removed we are from the Holocaust the more likely that a version of it will repeat. An irony there, of course, for the longer we go without catastrophe, the more the evidence might suggest that men and women have learned a lesson. But there are too many ominous signs nurturing unthinkable thoughts for that optimism to rest easy. There was a time, says Wiesel, when he believed that the Holocaust itself was humanity's protection. No longer. Continued threats to the survival of an Israeli state constitute a threat to Jews everywhere, and so Wiesel now declares himself a Zionist as part of his conviction that solidarity is one meaning of Jewishness today.[2] Combined with urgency, anger is an element now increased in his concerns. Anger that builds in response to an escalating movement to tell even the surviving victims that Hitler gave no extermination orders and that the Holocaust did not happen. Protest against falsifying revisions of history—that ingredient is part of being a Jew today.

A JEW TODAY: As I write those words during Chanukah and a few weeks before Christmas, 1977, the polishing touches are put on Wiesel's *Four Hasidic Masters,* a study of struggles against melancholy carried on by Jewish teachers whose timelessness and timeliness are one and the same.[3] At the same time, Marion Wiesel finishes the English translation of *Un Juif, Aujourd'hui.*[4] The portrait of a grandfather; a letter to a Palestinian Arab; reflections on Jerusalem; dialogues between a father and his son, a mother and her daughter, a man and his little sister; a plea for Holocaust survivors—these meditations form the vision of Jewishness that Elie Wiesel offers to American readers in 1978. They suggest what it can and should mean to be a Jew in the late twentieth century. They ask: who will be a Jew today?

One premise behind the lessons of *A Jew Today* is Wiesel's earlier statement "that to be a Jew means placing the accent on the verb *to be* and the noun *Jew* equally and simultaneously, to guard that one does not exclude the other or become fulfilled at the expense of the other. That to be a Jew means to serve God by taking sides with man and acting as his witness while affirming God's right to judge him. And, finally, that to be a Jew is to opt for God and creation alike— it is a refusal to oppose one to the other."[5] Substitute "Christian" for "Jew." The equation works again.

Within Wiesel's framework of refusal, the authentic Jew is one who opposes every power—divine and human—that threatens the sanctity of human life and thwarts compassion. This opposition for the sake of reconciliation rests on the recognition that life is a gift given to be chosen well and judged by the use we make of it. Further confessional commitments and theological beliefs—or the lack of them—are not the heart of the matter. They do have their place insofar as they provide orientation for caring. But more to the point is the degree to which one's name is a blessing: " 'You will know them by their fruits.' " (Matt. 7:16)

Jesus told the woman by the well that " 'salvation is from the Jews.' " What did he mean? Traditionally Christians understand that proclamation as a self-reference to Jesus. Centuries of opposition contest around that interpretation, and now, if ever, is surely the time to put exclusive and triumphal claims aside. That latter proposition does not mean that Christians should give up special loyalty to Jesus, any more than it means that Jews ought to start affirming that the Messiah has come. Jewish protest that he has *not* is crucial. It ought to intensify Christian feeling that a second coming is imperative—the only questions being whether this work, to the degree that it will occur at all, is left to human lives; or whether God himself will intervene again in history; or whether the Messiah truly comes, first or second, only with death and resurrection. And yet in a way those questions are no questions at all, because if anything is clear for now it is that Jews and Christians *together* have their work cut out for them. More than Yahweh—or should we say *along with God?*—the destructive events of our times reveal land, physical and spiritual, that requires us to leave behind old killing ways and to strive for healing.

Salvation comes from no single human individual or group alone, but insofar as men and women can make it happen on earth, those who serve God by taking sides for love, justice, and peace are indispensable. Salvation can come from Jews. It can also come from Christians, especially from those who are Jewish—as Jewish as the Master they follow, if not more so. *Who is a Jew today?* In one sense only those who share the memory, plight, and promise of a particular people, Israel. In another, any person who will share in Elie Wiesel's ultimate refusal to oppose God and creation to each other. Jewish Jews. Jewish Christians. Christian Christians. Maybe even Christian Jews, if the accent stays on the teachings of Jesus and not on doctrines about him. Calls for stands like those are messages that can and should be heard in sound testimony that salvation is from the Jews.

It is said that when a non-Jew expresses interest in becoming Jewish, that person should be asked: what reason have you for this choice of life; do you not know that the people of Israel are persecuted, oppressed, afflicted? I know and yet I desire to be a Jew—only if that reply is forthcoming should the person be accepted. But to what end? For what goals? So that persecution, oppression, affliction are opposed, refused the final say. The circumstances are not identical for one who seeks to be a Christian, but solidarity with Jews is firm for Christians in this way: to lift a cross and to follow Jesus only makes sense as an act of identification with the persecuted, oppressed, and afflicted. It does so, moreover, only if the aim is to see that persecution, oppression, affliction are opposed, refused the final say.

Making yokes easier, burdens lighter. When a Christian takes on the difficulty and weight of those tasks, he or she moves toward being a Jew today. That designation is not the only way to speak, and the point could also be made that as Jews carry out their calling to love justice and mercy they are working in the spirit of Jesus shared by authentic Christians. But for once, for now, forever, let the point for Christians be: learn to be a Jew today. Learn that to be a Jew today is not to make the world Jewish or Christian. Learn that the task is to be Jewish, to be Christian, to live, so as to humanize the world— and to die trying.

Notes

Preface

[1]G. F. W. Hegel, *Reason in History,* trans. Robert S. Hartman (Indianapolis: The Bobbs-Merrill Co., 1953), p. 27.

[2]Irving Greenberg, "Cloud of Smoke, Pillar of Fire: Judaism, Christianity, and Modernity After the Holocaust," in Eva Fleischner, ed., *Auschwitz: Beginning of a New Era?* (New York: KTAV Publishing House, Inc., 1977), p. 23.

Chapter I

[1]See Harry James Cargas, *Harry James Cargas in Conversation with Elie Wiesel* (New York: Paulist Press, 1976), p. 87. This book is a rich source of information about Wiesel and his authorship. Mrs. Molly Abramowitz also makes important contributions along these lines. See her *Elie Wiesel: A Bibliography* (Metuchen: The Scarecrow Press, Inc., 1974).

[2]Albert Camus, *The Rebel,* trans. Anthony Bower (New York: Vintage Books, 1956), p. 297.

[3]See Lucy S. Dawidowicz, *The War Against the Jews 1933–1945* (New York: Bantam Books, 1976), pp. xxiv–xxv.

[4]From Wiesel's opening night lecture, "Art and Culture After the Holocaust," given at the International Symposium on the Holocaust held at the Cathedral of St. John the Divine, New York City, June 3–6, 1974. The lecture is reprinted in Eva Fleischner, ed., *Auschwitz: Beginning of a New Era?* pp. 403–415. See especially p. 413.

[5]The quoted statement is from George Santayana, *The Life of Reason* (New York: Charles Scribner's Sons, 1954), p. 82. The book was originally published as five volumes in 1905–1906. The passage cited here is from Volume I, *Reason in Common Sense.*

[6]Elie Wiesel, "Talking and Writing and Keeping Silent," in Franklin H. Littell and Hubert G. Locke, eds., *The German Church Struggle and the Holocaust* (Detroit: Wayne State University Press, 1974), p. 269.

[7]*Harry James Cargas in Conversation with Elie Wiesel,* p. 3.

[8]Elie Wiesel, *The Oath,* trans. Marion Wiesel (New York: Random House, 1973), p. 154. Originally published as *Le Serment de Kolvillàg* (1973).

[9]Throughout this book, page numbers in parentheses refer to sources previously cited.

[10]See *Harry James Cargas in Conversation with Elie Wiesel,* p. 75.

[11] *Ibid.*, p. 75.
[12] *Ibid.*, p. 70.

Chapter II

[1] One basic bibliography, edited by Jacob Robinson and Philip Friedman, is the *Guide to Jewish History Under Nazi Impact* (New York: YIVO Institute for Jewish Research, 1960). It contains more than 3,500 entries covering many aspects of the Holocaust. In recent years, the number of Holocaust-related books released by American publishers has increased substantially. A spectrum includes: Howard Blum, *Wanted! The Search for Nazis in America* (New York: Quadrangle/The New York Times Book Company, 1976); Lucy S. Dawidowicz, *The War Against the Jews 1933–1945* (New York: Bantam Books, 1976); Terrence Des Pres, *The Survivor* (New York: Oxford University Press, 1976); Lawrence L. Langer, *The Holocaust and the Literary Imagination* (New Haven: Yale University Press, 1975); Dorothy Rabinowitz, *New Lives: Survivors of the Holocaust Living in America* (New York: Alfred A. Knopf, 1976); Richard L. Rubenstein, *The Cunning of History* (New York: Harper & Row, 1975); Albert Speer, *Spandau: The Secret Diaries* (New York: Pocket Books, 1977); and Simon Wiesenthal, *The Sunflower* (New York: Schocken Books, 1976).

[2] Three areas of controversy are crucial. All are related; each impinges on every person now alive, even as some dimensions have special significance for Jewish and Christian identities. One area is psychological. Was Jewish behavior in crisis and extremity characterized by passivity, nonresistance, and even regression to infantile patterns? Works such as Raul Hilberg's *The Destruction of the European Jews* (New York: Franklin Watts, Inc., 1973) and Bruno Bettelheim's *The Informed Heart* (New York: Avon Books, 1971) make cases for the affirmative. Dawidowicz's *The War Against the Jews 1933–1945* and Des Pres's *The Survivor* counter them, the latter also arguing that far from being an individual battle for survival-of-the-fittest, life in the camps often displayed communal concern of remarkable heights.

A second concern is ethical-political. It revolves around the question: Who bears responsibility? Important analyses include: Hannah Arendt, *Eichmann in Jerusalem* (New York: The Viking Press, 1973); Karl Jaspers, *The Question of German Guilt,* trans. E. B. Ashton (New York: Capricorn Books, 1961); Arthur D. Morse, *While Six Million Died* (New York: Hart Publishing Company, 1968); and Bradley Smith, *Reaching Judgment at Nuremberg* (New York: Basic Books, 1976).

The third dimension is religious. What role, if any, did God play in the Holocaust, and is faith in God warranted after Auschwitz? A range of contemporary Jewish responses includes: Richard Rubenstein's *After Auschwitz* (Indianapolis: The Bobbs-Merrill Company, 1966); Emil Fackenheim's *God's Presence in History* (New York: Harper Torchbooks, 1972); and Eliezer Berkovits's *Faith After the Holocaust* (New York: KTAV Publishing House, Inc., 1973). Christian responses in the United States, too few in number, tend thus far to focus on the Christian roots of anti-Semitism and on the Holocaust's implications for contemporary Christology. In these areas the works of A. Roy and Alice Eckardt, Edward H. Flannery, Thomas A. Idinopulos, Franklin H. Littell, Rosemary R. Ruether, Michael B. McGarry, and Paul M. van Buren are important. Signs of increasing thought by American Christians about the Holocaust are in the air, but it remains to be seen how that trend will develop and what practical impact it will have.

Two final bibliographical notes in this context. One of the Holocaust accounts most widely read in America in the 1970s has been Corrie ten Boom's *The Hiding Place* (Old Tappan, N.J.: Fleming H. Revell, 1971). This book is the autobiography of a Dutch Christian who helped to hide Jews from the Nazis. She narrowly escaped death in the Ravensbrück concentration camp. Her writings receive much attention among evangelical Christians in the United States. Finally, although a report on European theological responses to the Holocaust cannot be given here, a worthwhile overview of the recent scene in Germany is offered by Alice and Roy Eckardt in their article, "How German Thinkers View the Holocaust," published in the March 17, 1976, issue of *The Christian Century*, pp. 249–252. In this conjunction see also A. Roy Eckardt, "Jürgen Moltmann, the Jewish People, and the Holocaust," in *Journal of the American Academy of Religion*, December 1976, pp. 675–691.

[3]My historical outline of Holocaust events relies extensively on the following works: Dawidowicz, *The War Against the Jews 1933–1945;* Hilberg, *The Destruction of the European Jews;* Nora Levin, *The Holocaust* (New York: Schocken Books, 1973); Judah Pilch, ed., *The Jewish Catastrophe in Europe* (New York: The American Association for Jewish Education, 1968); and a 1975 publication, *The Holocaust,* produced by Yad Vashem/Martyrs' and Heroes' Remembrance Authority, Jerusalem. Hilberg's book, published originally in 1961, remains the definitive scholarly history. The author, a political scientist, concentrates more on the Nazis than on the Jewish victims. The other works mentioned here tip the balance the other way.

[4]Hilberg cites a figure of one million; Dawidowicz doubles it. See *The Destruction of the European Jews,* p. 572, and *The War Against the Jews 1933–1945,* pp. 199–200. One source, the Committee to Investigate Nazi Crimes, places the estimate at 2.4 to 4 million. See Jacob Glatstein, Israel Knox, and Samuel Margoshes, eds., *Anthology of Holocaust Literature* (New York: Atheneum Press, 1975), pp. 176–177.

[5]Himmler was *Reichsführer* for the SS (*Schutzstaffeln,* Defense Corps). Its units were responsible for guarding Nazi leaders, stifling resistance, and operating the concentration camps. Himmler was from a Catholic background. He modeled the SS after Jesuit organizational patterns.

[6]See *The War Against the Jews 1933–1945,* p. 63. In 1932, five elections were held in the crumbling Weimar Republic. The one on November 6 is significant because it was the last before Hitler took power. In this election the Nazis actually lost 34 seats in the *Reichstag* (German

parliament). They never achieved an absolute majority in any free national election.

[7]See *The War Against the Jews 1933–1945,* especially pp. 142–148.

[8]See pp. 47–48 below. Hilberg discusses the definition problem at length. See *The Destruction of the European Jews,* especially pp. 43–53.

[9]Examples of New Testament texts used to support the "teaching of contempt" include: Mark 14:1, 11, 43 ff., 55, 64; 15:11–15; Matthew 23; 27 —28; Luke 23:18–31; John 5:16–18; 6:41; 7:1, 13; 8:42–47; 10:31; 19; Acts 7:51–60; 1 Thessalonians 2:13–16; Revelation 2:9. For more detail on the early Christian roots of anti-Semitism, see Rosemary R. Ruether, *Faith and Fratricide* (New York: Seabury Press, 1974); Thomas A. Idinopulos and Roy Bowen Ward, "Is Christology Inherently Anti-Semitic?: A Critical Review of Rosemary Ruether's *Faith and Fratricide,"* in *Journal of the American Academy of Religion,* June 1977, pp. 193–214; A. Roy Eckardt, *Your People, My People* (New York: Quadrangle/The New York Times Book Company, 1974); Edward H. Flannery, *The Anguish of the Jews* (New York: Macmillan, 1965); Franklin H. Littell, *The Crucifixion of the Jews* (New York: Harper & Row, 1975); and Paul M. van Buren, *The Burden of Freedom* (New York: Seabury Press, 1976).

[10]Quoted from Dawidowicz, *The War Against the Jews 1933–1945,* p. 29. Hilberg cites similar passages from Luther. See *The Destruction of the European Jews,* pp. 8–13. The usual source for Luther's hostile comments on the Jews is his treatise "On the Jews and Their Lies" (1543). See *Luther's Works,* Vol. 47, *The Christian in Society* (St. Louis: Fortress Press, 1958), pp. 121–306. Noting that "the Jews have suffered immensely because of this treatise," Aarne Siirala presents an informative discussion of this writing and its publication. See his "Reflections from a Lutheran Perspective," in *Auschwitz: Beginning of a New Era?,* pp. 135–148.

[11]Richard L. Rubenstein's *The Cunning of History* deserves wide reading in this regard. Subtitled "Mass Death and the American Future," it offers warnings no less important than they are grim. And grim they are. Rubenstein argues persuasively that the factors which spawned the Holocaust are alive and well today, not least in the United States. Indeed the advance of civilization has made human life so abundant that it is more superfluous, cumbersome, and therefore dispensable, than ever. Moreover, available to us are techniques for organization and disposal of human life far more sophisticated and efficient than the Nazis possessed. All we need is the will to mobilize them, and the future—American and/or human—could be one of mass death. Rubenstein is a gambler. He knows that "thinking the worst possible case," as he calls it, is risky business. Doing so may have the unintended consequences of nourishing the wrong ideas in the wrong minds and of turning prophecy into its own fulfillment. But Rubenstein takes the chance that his warnings may be heeded by better men and women and thereby that worst possible cases may be forestalled. One way or another all of us are determining which bet wins.

[12]An indispensable record on this point is provided by Arthur D. Morse's *While Six Million Died.* Morse, a long-time reporter-director for CBS News, subtitles his book "A Chronicle of American Apathy." He concludes his Introduction with these words: "If genocide is to be prevented in the future, we must understand how it happened in the past—not only in terms of the killers and the killed *but of the bystanders.*" (My emphasis.)

[13]Quoted from Levin, *The Holocaust,* p. 6.

[14]Major transportation networks were needed to utilize these new killing centers. Thus, the sites were selected not only with an eye on the large centers of Jewish population in Eastern Europe but also on convenient rail facilities. Auschwitz, for instance, was on the main route between Vienna and Krakow.

[15]See n. 2 above.

[16]See Pilch, ed., *The Jewish Catastrophe in Europe,* p. 66.

[17]Even in death camps such as Auschwitz, there were non-Jewish inmates: German criminals, social rejects, and political prisoners, Poles, Slavs, Gypsies and Christians. German prisoners especially tended to receive milder treatment than Jews. They often occupied supervisory positions. Jews could expect no assistance or comfort from them, because the lives of such overseers depended on strict enforcement of Nazi policy. On the other hand, even the most scrupulous fulfillment of responsibilities by an inmate-supervisor was no guarantee of survival. For example, *Kapos*—occasionally a Jew among them —might live better for a while, but after a few months they also could be sent to death.

[18]See especially Des Pres, *The Survivor.*

[19]Leo Eitinger, *Concentration Camp Survivors in Norway and Israel* (London: Allen & Unwin, 1964), p. 80. Eitinger was captured by the Nazis in Norway, imprisoned, and eventually deported to Auschwitz. His research and writing continue.

[20]See the *New York Times,* Thursday, January 20, 1977, p. 12. The following lines from the letter are significant. "Are you surprised the world responded with dismay and outrage?" Wiesel asks President Giscard d'Estaing. "Your own people rose to speak out against you. Because while you have visited Auschwitz, you have forgotten its lesson."

Chapter III

[1]Elie Wiesel, *Night,* trans. Stella Rodway (New York: Avon Books, 1969), p. 40. Originally published as *La Nuit* (1958). The first American edition appeared in 1960.

[2]Elie Wiesel, *One Generation After,* trans. Lily Edelman and the author (New York: Avon Books, 1972), p. 216. Originally published as *Entre deux soliels* (1970). The first American edition also appeared in 1970.

[3]Elie Wiesel, *Dawn,* trans. Frances Frenaye (New York: Avon Books, 1970), p. 24. Originally published as *L'Aube* (1960). The first American edition appeared in 1961. Elie Wiesel has said that "I'm very careful with names. I choose names prudently; they always have a certain meaning, a

special meaning to me." (See *Harry James Cargas in Conversation with Elie Wiesel,* p. 50. Professor Michael Berenbaum of Wesleyan University has also helped me to understand the significance of names in Wiesel's writings.) Often the main characters in Wiesel's books bear names that are variants of "El," meaning God. Elisha ("God will save") is an example, as is Michael ("who is like God") in *The Town Beyond the Wall.*

The point of this naming is to underscore the links and tensions between God and human persons. Human identity involves God, but that fact creates as many problems as it solves. Turning the names "Elisha" and "Michael" into questions drives that truth home. But not only God is involved in names. Jewish ancestors—and even angels—play a role, too. The Elisha of *Dawn,* for instance, harks back to a biblical prophet, the successor to Elijah, and to Elisha ben Abuyah, a Jewish heretic who reputedly affirmed that the world is without justice and without a judge. Such images, and the issues they raise, also cast forward: Wiesel's son is named Elisha.

[4]*Harry James Cargas in Conversation with Elie Wiesel,* p. 18.

[5]Elie Wiesel, *The Accident,* trans. Anne Borchardt (New York: Avon Books, 1970), p. 79. Originally published as *Le Jour* (1961). The first American edition appeared in 1962.

Chapter IV

[1]See *Elie Wiesel: A Small Measure of Victory* (Tucson: The University of Arizona, 1974), p. 17. This booklet contains interviews with Wiesel by Professors Gene Koppel and Henry Kaufman of the University of Arizona. The interviews were held on April 25, 1973.

[2]Elie Wiesel, "From Holocaust to Rebirth." This statement is taken from a reprint of Wiesel's Herbert R. Abeles Memorial Address, delivered at the 39th General Assembly of the Council of Jewish Federations and Welfare Funds, November 14, 1970, at Kansas City, Missouri. See p. 4.

[3]Elie Wiesel, "Against Despair." This essay, published as a pamphlet by the United Jewish Appeal, is a reprint of the first annual Louis A. Pincus Memorial Lecture, which was delivered by Wiesel on December 8, 1973. See p. 11.

[4]Elie Wiesel, *The Gates of the Forest,* trans. Frances Frenaye (New York: Avon Books, 1972), Introduction. Originally published as *Les Portes de la forêt* (1964). The first American edition appeared in 1966.

[5]Elie Wiesel, *The Town Beyond the Wall,* trans. Stephen Becker (New York: Avon Books, 1970), p. 101. Originally published as *La Ville de la chance* (1962). The first American edition appeared in 1964.

[6]*Harry James Cargas in Conversation with Elie Wiesel,* p. 53.

[7]"Talking and Writing and Keeping Silent" in *The German Church Struggle and the Holocaust,* p. 271. Earlier, in 1967, Wiesel responded to comments from an audience by saying: "As for God, I did speak about Him. I do little else in my books." And he went on to add, "It's my problem, and His, too." See "Jewish Values in the Post-Holocaust Future: A Symposium," *Judaism*

16 (Summer 1967), p. 298. Along with Wiesel, Emil L. Fackenheim, Richard H. Popkin, and George Steiner were panelists in this important discussion.

⁸*Harry James Cargas in Conversation with Elie Wiesel,* p. 52.

⁹*Ibid.,* p. 52.

¹⁰Elie Wiesel, *A Beggar in Jerusalem,* trans. Lily Edelman and the author (New York: Avon Books, 1971), p. 244. Originally published as *Le Mendiant de Jérusalem* (1968). The first American edition appeared in 1970.

¹¹Elie Wiesel, *Legends of Our Time,* trans. Steven Donadio (New York: Avon Books, 1972), p. viii. Originally published as *Le Chants des morts* (1966). The first American edition appeared in 1968.

¹²*Harry James Cargas in Conversation with Elie Wiesel,* p. 17.

¹³Professor Michael Berenbaum points out that Kolvillàg is formed from the Hebrew "kol," meaning "every," and from the Hungarian "villàg," meaning "village" or "town." Kolvillàg, then, can be viewed as a symbol for the countless Jewish communities in Eastern Europe that were destroyed by Holocaust flames, some with survivors and some with none at all. Part of the task that Wiesel sets himself as a writer is to bring destroyed towns and persons back into life through his writings. To succeed in that effort against the vast successes of the Nazis in the destruction of European Jewry is at least a small measure of victory against them. A bush was burned up—almost, but not completely.

¹⁴See Yuri Suhl, ed., *They Fought Back* (New York: Schocken Books, 1975), pp. 128–135. The pages cited recount the experiences of Samuel Rajzman, a participant in the revolt at Treblinka and one of the few Jews to survive it.

Chapter V

¹From Wiesel's keynote address at a Symposium on Revolutions in Culture and the Arts, held at the Graduate School of the City University of New York. The talk is published in *Revolutionary Directions in Intellectual and Cultural Production: Their Consequences for the Higher Learning* (New York: Research Foundation of the City University of New York, 1975). See especially p. 78.

²Quoted from a pamphlet prepared by the Holocaust Memorial Committee, New Haven, Connecticut, April 1977.

³Wiesel expressed such feelings to me in a conversation on November 28, 1975.

⁴Elie Wiesel, *The Jews of Silence,* trans. Neal Kozodoy (New York: Signet Books, 1967), p. vii. The essays in this volume first appeared as a series of articles for the Israeli newspaper, *Yediot Aharanot.* The book version was originally published as *Les Juifs du silence* (1966). The first American edition also appeared in 1966.

⁵See the First Louis L. Kaplan Convocation Lecture, given by Elie Wiesel on October 23, 1973, published in pamphlet form by the Baltimore Hebrew College, p. 10.

⁶*Harry James Cargas in Conversation with Elie Wiesel*, p. 31.

⁷Speaking in another place about the Holocaust and God's covenant with Israel, Wiesel says: "Well, it seems that, for the first time in our history, this very covenant was broken. That is why the Holocaust has terrifying theological implications. Whether we want it or not, because of its sheer dimensions, the event transcends man and involves more than him alone. *It can be explained neither with God nor without Him.*" (My emphasis.) See "Jewish Values in the Post-Holocaust Future: A Symposium," p. 281.

⁸Elie Wiesel, "Two Images, One Destiny." This essay, published as a pamphlet by the United Jewish Appeal, is a reprint of a talk given by Wiesel at The Jewish Agency Assembly in Jerusalem, June 1974. See p. 13 of the pamphlet.

⁹Elie Wiesel, *Zalmen, or the Madness of God*, trans. Nathan Edelman (New York: Random House, 1974), p. 53. This work was adapted for the stage by Marion Wiesel. Produced first by French national radio, the play had its world premiere in English in Washington, D.C., May 1974. The text was originally published as *Zalmen ou la folie de Dieu* (1968). The first American edition appeared in 1974.

¹⁰The communal chanting of *Kol Nidre* evokes the memory of past persecution, declares null and void vows between an individual and God made under duress, and renews faith that has faltered.

¹¹Biblical references about God's power that are important in this context include the following: Genesis 18:14; Job 42:2; Jeremiah 32:17; Mark 10:27 and Luke 1:37.

Chapter VI

¹See also Psalm 34:15–16.

²Elie Wiesel, *Souls on Fire: Portraits and Legends of Hasidic Masters*, trans. Marion Wiesel (New York: Random House, 1972), p. 209. Originally published as *Célébration hassidique, portraits et légendes* (1972).

³Elie Wiesel, *Ani Maamin: A Song Lost and Found Again*, trans. Marion Wiesel (New York: Random House, 1973), p. 11. The French text is printed in the volume cited, which is the original edition of this work.

⁴Elie Wiesel, *Messengers of God: Biblical Portraits and Legends*, trans. Marion Wiesel (New York: Random House, 1976), p. 28. Originally published as *Célébration biblique, portraits et légendes* (1976).

⁵The dialogue quoted here is attributed to Rebbe Menahem-Mendl of Kotzk and one of his disciples. I set the lines in a context different from the one reported by Elie Wiesel. For comparison see *Messengers of God*, pp. 35–36.

⁶*Harry James Cargas in Conversation with Elie Wiesel*, p. 80.

⁷In Wiesel's telling of the tale, he adds the following words: "Had Cain spoken thus, how different history would have turned out!" The suggestion is that if Cain had spoken this way, there would have been no murder. My account takes another step, perhaps pushing Wiesel's idea farther.

[8]See two books by Alfred North Whitehead: *Religion in the Making* (Cleveland: Meridian Books, 1965), p. 148; and *Process and Reality* (New York: Harper Torchbooks, 1960), p. 526.

[9]*Harry James Cargas in Conversation with Elie Wiesel,* pp. 19, 20.

[10]The confessional language quoted here, and in the sentences that follow, is taken from *The Book of Confessions* (Second Edition, 1970) of The United Presbyterian Church in the United States of America. Specifically, I quote from "The Confession of 1967." The quoted statements express beliefs that most American Christians would accept. Using the reference system employed in *The Book of Confessions,* the passages quoted are found in paragraphs 9.13, 9.07, 9.09, 9.15, 9.19, and 9.32.

An Epilogue

[1]See Morton A. Reichek, "Elie Wiesel: Out of the Night," in *Present Tense,* Spring 1976, pp. 41–47, and especially p. 47. This interview-article contains extensive statements by Wiesel himself.

[2]See Elie Wiesel, "Ominous Signs and Unthinkable Thoughts," in *ADL Bulletin,* April 1975, p. 7. Also see Elie Wiesel, "The Honor of Being a Zionist," in *The Jewish Community Bulletin,* January 1976, p. 8. The latter piece is reprinted from *Le Figaro,* Paris, by the Jewish Federation-Council of Greater Los Angeles.

[3]This work is published by the University of Notre Dame Press, Notre Dame, Indiana, 1978.

[4]*Un Juif, Aujourd'hui* was originally published in 1977 by Éditions du Seuil, Paris.

[5]Elie Wiesel, " 'Hear, O Israel,' " in Merle Severy, ed., *Great Religions of the World* (Washington, D. C.: National Geographic Society, 1971), p. 177.

Selected Bibliography

I.

Books by Elie Wiesel (listed in order of first American editions)

Night, trans. Stella Rodway. New York: Hill and Wang, 1960.
Dawn, trans. Anne Borchardt. New York: Hill and Wang, 1961.
The Accident, trans. Anne Borchardt. New York: Hill and Wang, 1962.
The Town Beyond the Wall, trans. Steven Becker. New York: Atheneum, 1964.
The Gates of the Forest, trans. Frances Frenaye. New York: Holt, Rinehart and Winston, 1966.
The Jews of Silence, trans. Neal Kozodoy. New York: Holt, Rinehart and Winston, 1966.
Legends of Our Time, trans. Steven Donadio. New York: Holt, Rinehart and Winston, 1968.
A Beggar in Jerusalem, trans. Lily Edelman and the author. New York: Random House, 1970.
One Generation After, trans. Lily Edelman and the author. New York: Random House, 1970.
Souls on Fire, trans. Marion Wiesel. New York: Random House, 1972.
The Oath, trans. Marion Wiesel. New York: Random House, 1973.
Ani Maamin, trans. Marion Wiesel. New York: Random House, 1973.
Zalmen, or the Madness of God, trans. Nathan Edelman. New York: Random House, 1974.
Messengers of God, trans. Marion Wiesel. New York: Random House, 1976.
Four Hasidic Masters, Notre Dame: University of Notre Dame Press, 1978.
A Jew Today, trans. Marion Wiesel. New York: Random House, 1978.

II.

Some Articles by Elie Wiesel (listed in order of publication and limited to those quoted in this book)

"From Holocaust to Rebirth." New York: The Council of Jewish Federations and Welfare Funds, 1970.
" 'Hear, O Israel.' " Merle Severy, ed., *Great Religions of the World.* Washington, D.C.: National Geographic Society, 1971.
"First Louis L. Kaplan Convocation Lecture." Baltimore: Baltimore Hebrew College, 1973.
"Against Despair." New York: United Jewish Appeal, 1973.
"Two Images, One Destiny." New York: United Jewish Appeal, 1974.

"Talking and Writing and Keeping Silent." Franklin H. Littell and Hubert G. Locke, eds., *The German Church Struggle and the Holocaust.* Detroit: Wayne State University Press, 1974.

"Ominous Signs and Unthinkable Thoughts." New York: *ADL Bulletin,* April 1975.

"Keynote Address for the Symposium on Revolutions in Culture and the Arts." *Revolutionary Directions in Intellectual and Cultural Production.* New York: Research Foundation of the City University of New York, 1975.

"The Honor of Being a Zionist." Los Angeles: *The Jewish Community Bulletin,* January 1976.

"Art and Culture After the Holocaust." Eva Fleischner, ed., *Auschwitz: Beginning of a New Era?* New York: KTAV Publishing House, Inc., 1977.

III.
Published Discussions and Interviews with Elie Wiesel

Cargas, Harry James. *Harry James Cargas in Conversation with Elie Wiesel.* New York: Paulist Press, 1976.

"Jewish Values in the Post-Holocaust Future: A Symposium." *Judaism.* Summer 1967.

Koppel, Gene and Henry Kaufman. *Elie Wiesel: A Small Measure of Victory.* Tucson: The University of Arizona, 1974.

Reichek, Morton A. "Elie Wiesel: Out of the Night." *Present Tense,* Spring 1976.

IV.
Some Significant Books and Articles That Deal with Elie Wiesel and/or the Holocaust
(Most of the editions listed are among those currently in print, not necessarily the original editions)

Abramowitz, Molly. *Elie Wiesel: A Bibliography.* Metuchen: The Scarecrow Press, Inc., 1974.

Arendt, Hannah. *Eichmann in Jerusalem.* New York: The Viking Press, 1963.

Arendt, Hannah. *The Origins of Totalitarianism,* rev. ed. New York: Harcourt Brace, 1966.

Berenbaum, Michael G. "Elie Wiesel and Contemporary Jewish Theology." *Conservative Judaism.* Spring 1976.

Berenbaum, Michael G. *Elie Wiesel: The Vision of the Void.* Middletown: Wesleyan University Press, forthcoming.

Berkovits, Eliezer. *Faith After the Holocaust.* New York: KTAV Publishing House, Inc., 1973.

Bettelheim, Bruno. *The Informed Heart.* New York: Avon Books, 1971.

Blum, Howard. *Wanted! The Search for Nazis in America.* New York: Quadrangle/The New York Times Book Company, 1976.

Brown, Robert McAfee. "The Holocaust as a Problem in Moral Choice." *Dimensions of the Holocaust.* Evanston: Northwestern University, 1977.

Camus, Albert. *The Rebel,* trans. Anthony Bower. New York: Vintage Books, 1956.

Cargas, Harry James. *The Holocaust: An Annotated Bibliography.* Haverford: The Catholic Library Association, 1977.

Cargas, Harry James, ed. *Responses to Elie Wiesel.* New York: Persea Books, 1978.

Dawidowicz, Lucy S. *The War Against the Jews 1933–1945.* New York: Bantam Books, 1976.

Des Pres, Terrence. *The Survivor.* New York: Oxford University Press, 1976.

Eckardt, A. Roy. "Jürgen Moltmann, the Jewish People, and the Holocaust." *Journal of the American Academy of Religion.* December 1976.

Eckardt, A. Roy. *Your People, My People.* New York: Quadrangle/The New York Times Book Company, 1974.

Eckardt, Alice and A. Roy Eckardt. "German Thinkers View the Holocaust." *The Christian Century,* March 17, 1976.

Eitinger, Leo. *Concentration Camp Survivors in Norway and Israel.* London: Allen & Unwin, 1964.

Fackenheim, Emil. *God's Presence in History.* New York: Harper Torchbooks, 1972.

Flannery, Edward H. *The Anguish of the Jews.* New York: Macmillan, 1965.

Fleischner, Eva, ed. *Auschwitz: Beginning of a New Era?* New York: KTAV Publishing House, Inc., 1977.

Friedlander, Albert H., ed. *Out of the Whirlwind.* New York: Schocken Books, 1976.

Friedman, Maurice. *The Hidden Human Image.* New York: Delacorte Press, 1974.

Friedman, Maurice. *To Deny Our Nothingness.* New York: Delacorte Press, 1967.

Glatstein, Jacob, Israel Knox and Samuel Margoshes, eds. *Anthology of Holocaust Literature.* New York: Atheneum, 1975.

Greenberg, Irving and Alvin Rosenfeld, eds. *Confronting the Holocaust: The Impact of Elie Wiesel.* Bloomington: Indiana University Press, forthcoming.

Halperin, Irving. *Messengers from the Dead.* Philadelphia: The Westminster Press, 1970.

Hilberg, Raul. *The Destruction of the European Jews.* New York: Franklin Watts, Inc., 1973.

The Holocaust. Jerusalem: Yad Vashem, 1975.

Idinopulos, Thomas A. and Roy Bowen Ward. "Is Christology Inherently Anti-Semitic?: A Critical Review of Rosemary Ruether's *Faith and Fratricide.*" *Journal of the American Academy of Religion.* June 1977.

Idinopulos, Thomas A. "The Holocaust in the Stories of Elie Wiesel." *Soundings.* Summer 1972.

Jaspers, Karl. *The Question of German Guilt,* trans. E. B. Ashton. New York: Capricorn Books, 1961.

Jung, C. K. *Answer to Job,* trans. R. F. C. Hull. Princeton: Princeton University Press, 1973.

Knopp, Josephine. *The Trial of Judaism in Contemporary Jewish Writing.* Urbana: University of Illinois Press, 1974.

Knopp, Josephine. "Wiesel and the Absurd." *Contemporary Literature.* April 1974.

Langer, Lawrence L. *The Holocaust and the Literary Imagination.* New Haven: Yale University Press, 1975.

Levin, Nora. *The Holocaust.* New York: Schocken Books, 1975.

Littell, Franklin H. *The Crucifixion of the Jews.* New York: Harper & Row, 1975.

Littell, Franklin H. and Hubert G. Locke, eds. *The German Church Struggle and the Holocaust.* Detroit: Wayne State University Press, 1974.

McGarry, Michael B. *Christology After Auschwitz.* New York: Paulist Press, 1977.

Morse, Arthur D. *While Six Million Died.* New York: Hart Publishing Company, 1968.

Pilch, Judah, ed. *The Jewish Catastrophe in Europe.* New York: The American Association for Jewish Education, 1968.

Rabinowitz, Dorothy. *New Lives: Survivors of the Holocaust Living in America.* New York: Alfred A. Knopf, 1976.

Robinson, Jacob and Philip Friedman, eds. *Guide to Jewish History Under Nazi Impact.* New York: YIVO Institute for Jewish Research, 1960.

Roth, John K. "Nothing Was the Same Again: A Meditation on the Holocaust, Elie Wiesel's *Messengers of God,* and American Experience." Klaus Lanzinger, ed., *Americana-Austriaca,* Vol. 4. Vienna: Wilhelm Braumüller, 1978.

Roth, John K. "Tears and Elie Wiesel." *The Princeton Seminary Bulletin.* December 1972.

Roth, John K. "Turns of Fortune: Reflections on Elie Wiesel and *The Oath.*" Sy M. Kahn and Martha Raetz, eds., *Interculture.* Vienna: Wilhelm Braümuller, 1975.

Rubenstein, Richard L. *After Auschwitz.* Indianapolis: The Bobbs-Merrill Company, 1966.

Rubenstein, Richard L. *The Cunning of History.* New York: Harper & Row, 1975.

Rubenstein, Richard L. "Job and Auschwitz." *Union Seminary Quarterly Review.* Summer 1970.

Ruether, Rosemary R. *Faith and Fratricide.* New York: Seabury Press, 1974.

Sherwin, Byron L. "Elie Wiesel and Jewish Theology." *Judaism.* Winter 1969.

Smith, Bradley. *Reaching Judgment at Nuremberg.* New York: Basic Books, 1976.

Speer, Albert. *Spandau: The Secret Diaries.* New York: Pocket Books, 1976.

Suhl, Yuri, ed. *They Fought Back.* New York: Schocken Books, 1975.

ten Boom, Corrie. *The Hiding Place.* Old Tappan: Fleming H. Revell, 1971.

Tiefel, Hans O. "Holocaust Interpretations and Religious Assumptions." *Judaism.* Spring 1976.

van Buren, Paul M. *The Burden of Freedom.* New York: Seabury Press, 1976.

Wiesenthal, Simon. *The Sunflower.* New York: Schocken Books, 1976.